Visualising
Information
for Advocacy

TACTICAL
TECHNOLOGY
COLLECTIVE

tacticaltech.org

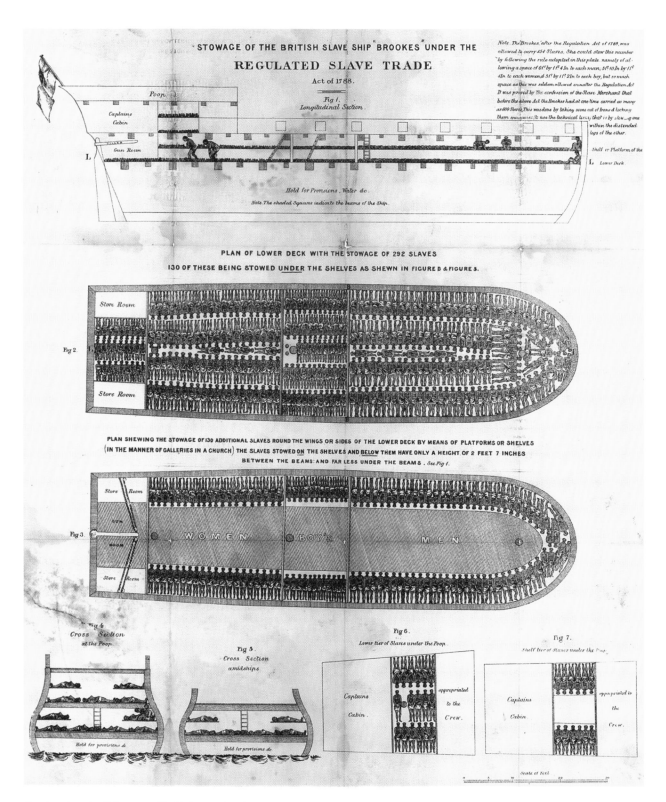

Brookes slave ship 18th century, The Bridgeman Art Library.

Introduction

"Most prevalent disorders in negro-ships are fevers and dysentries; consequences of numbers being ill of the latter extremely noxious; can not conceive of any situation so dreadful and disgusting. In the *Alexander*, deck was covered with blood and mucus, resembled a slaughter-house; the stench and foul air were intolerable."

This evidence describing the conditions aboard the *Alexander*, a slave trade ship, was given by Alexander Falconbridge to the House of Commons in 1789.

A year earlier, the Plymouth Abolitionist movement in the United Kingdom had commissioned a sketch of the *Brookes*, a slave ship like the one described by Falconbridge. The London based *Society for Effecting the Abolition of the Slave Trade*, seeing how powerful this image was, picked up the idea and commissioned a more detailed engraving, circulating it on 7,000 posters. James Philips, who owned a publishing and printing business in London, had got the information about the "stowage of slaves" through his Quaker networks, and by gaining access to official documents from the Liverpool Customs office. Much as today's activists do, Thomas Clarkson and the other members of the Society for Effecting the Abolition of the Slave Trade relied on access to **information**, on the **design** of that information, on extensive **networks**, and on **technologies** of distribution to deploy their campaign.

What the Plymouth Abolitionist Committee chose to present was a diagram of the ship's lower planking and 'poop deck'. The posters showed how people were packed like cargo into the ship, forced to lie on their sides and unable to stand for up to six months at a time. The poster also carried an account from a slave trader who confessed to carrying as many as 609 slaves at one time, 155 people more than the *Brookes* allowed for, according to the schematic, thus implying that the conditions were really much worse even than those pictured. This image was to become a key asset for the campaign to abolish slavery and would go down in history as testimony to the power

of visual evidence. Looking at the diagram now, curiosity trips over disbelief as you begin to imagine what this would have meant for those on board. A diagram like this one, that would normally be used to show how cargo may be packed on a ship, makes this depiction of humanity all the more horrific. You are left wondering: *how could they have done this?* If today this looks like a form of ancient brutality, then as a depiction of contemporary practices it must really have defied people's beliefs at the time. It strikes a note that is too loud to ignore.

In 1808 Thomas Clarkson wrote, about the history of the abolitionist movement: "... the print seemed to make an instantaneous impression of horror upon all who saw it, and was therefore instrumental, in consequence of the wide circulation given it, in serving the cause of the injured Africans".[1] When Clarkson took the poster to France, the Archbishop of Aix was reportedly so "struck with horror that he could scarcely speak".[2] These images shocked the viewer, but they also did something much more powerful. They showed how absurd these practices were.

The leaders of the Abolitionist movement made use of a range of visual formats as evidence to support their demands. The image of the *Brookes*, which was used as testimony in parliament, still today gives us a sense of facts merely presented, speaking for themselves in visual form.

At the same time, Thomas Clarkson and his network of activists had paintings commissioned, created children's books and had china crockery printed with the Abolitionist slogans *'Am I not a Man and a Brother?'*, *'Am I not a Woman and a Sister?'*

1   Thomas Clarkson in his History of the Rise, Progress, and Accomplishment of the Abolition of the African Slave Trade, Longman Hurst, Rees and Orme, London, 1808.
2   http://www.hullcc.gov.uk/museumcollections/collections/storydetail.php?irn=154&master=443

LEFT:
Anti-slavery jug, circa 1807.
Photograph by Leo Reynolds, 2009.

The images used on these objects were used to elicit feelings of outrage and sympathy – not by presenting facts, but by **representing** the perseverance of human dignity in the face of wretchedness and dehumanisation. On the china cup, for instance, we see the representation of the slave's isolation on the rocks, the distance of the sea and the restrictions of his chains contrasted with his enduring humanity. The slogan emphasises this demand for dignity, asking the viewer *"Am I not a Man and a Brother?"*. Ideas are not presented as facts, as in the schematic of the *Brookes*, but are represented pictorially and used as a call to action. The person using this cup to serve tea to visitors transformed a social act into an act of solidarity, making a statement of allegiance to the abolitionist cause.

Through these two examples we can recognise **two functions of visualising information for advocacy:** *presentation* **(the objective description of the facts) and** *representation* **(the subjective depiction of ideas through metaphor, analogy and allegory)**. In many campaign images these two functions are mixed, but it is important that we learn to understand them as separate elements of visual information, so that we can recognise in what measure each is working. This guide and the examples in it will explore the communicative power of each of these elements and how they are used in advocacy.

The anti-slavery campaign is often held up as the world's first social justice campaign[3], and it set precedents for campaigns today. The Abolitionists lobbied parliament with 1,500 petitions, signed by 1.5 million people; they organised 300,000 people in the UK in a boycott of sugar produced by slaves in the [British] West Indies. Over a twenty-year period they used all the tricks they could muster, from strategic alliances to direct lobbying, and from appeals to sentiment to calls to action.

On 12th May 1789, Wilberforce used a model replica of the *Brookes* to add weight to his argument in his speech to the House of Commons. Concluding the speech, Wilberforce said *"Having heard all of this you may choose to look the other way but you can never again say that you did not know"*.[4]

---

3   For an overview of the campaign, see Strategy in Information and Influence Campaigns: How Policy Advocates, Social Movements, Insurgent Groups, Corporations, Governments and Others Get What They Want, Jarol Manheim. Routledge, New York, 2011.

4   Try the film *Amazing Grace*, in which people flypost this image, though experts are likely to be put off by the Hollywood adaptation of the story, but it has its moments.

In this statement, Wilberforce made an appeal to the morality of his audience as well as to their sense of reason. What Wilberforce is actually saying is that once the facts have been seen the only rational conclusion to be reached is that slavery must be abolished. Thereafter, any failure to demand abolition can only signify irrationality (the inability to put the facts together in a logical order) or immorality (the willful desire to ignore them). Wilberforce presents three options to his audience: they must be either abolitionists, idiots or evil.

If we look at the techniques used by the abolitionists, we can identify three important and distinct elements of persuasion that are essential to visualising information for advocacy. The most familiar to us – the one that is still at the centre of our understanding of democracy – is **rational** argument. We use this to influence people because we believe that if they are provided with the true facts, their ability to reason will allow them to reach the right conclusion. The schematic of the *Brookes* is an example of this approach. It made people question their understanding of what slavery entailed. The second element of persuasion is **moral** appeal. This uses the (presumed) ethical convictions of the audience to recruit them or nudge them into taking a position, as the Abolitionists did with their representation of human integrity on the china cup. This approach makes an appeal to people's values and attempts to awaken their sense of justice and move them to act. The third element is **emotional** appeal. This form of persuasion tries to produce and exploit emotional reactions to gain the support of the audience. This can be seen in the anecdote about the Archbishop of Aix and his highly emotional reaction to the image of the *Brookes*. Emotional appeals seek to stir people's empathy and compassion regardless of underlying social norms and personal notions of justice and in this sense can be the most powerful of the three appeals. These three approaches – **rational appeal, moral appeal and emotional appeal**[5] – are three ways to persuade an audience. They are often used together.

The schematic of the *Brookes* appears to be purely factual, to be an objective presentation of slavery. In this case, the presentation of the facts encompasses all three forms of appeal: it invites people to think, appeals to their moral sense, and produces a strong emotional reaction. But although the image appears to contain simple facts that speak for themselves, we know that the schematic was commissioned. Therefore, what looks like a completely objective presentation is also a selective representation of the issue. This may seem overly analytical, but it raises crucial questions about ways of framing and using visual information: what are the choices the author makes about what to show and how to show it? How does the author position themselves with regard to the creation of the image?

How apparent is the framing of the information to the viewer? And to what degree does the viewer feel forced by this to reach a certain conclusion? These details have a significant impact on how an image influences people. In choosing the image of the *Brookes* mass-produced posters, Clarkson and Wilberforce made specific decisions and created a powerful visual shorthand to encapsulate the problem. While the injustice and suffering of those who endured the slave ships was brutal, the poster does not try to show the whole institution of slavery; in fact, the Middle Passage was not the central problem of the slave trade. The Abolitionists simplified the problem into a single story, one that they believed would convey as **fact** the horror and immorality of the entire practice.

Using these elements to decode the communicative power of the schematic of the *Brookes* allows us to reverse-engineer the elements of a successful visual information campaign. These same elements can be used to design powerful visual information for new campaigns. We wrote this guide to describe ways of creating persuasive visual information campaigns, campaigns that through representation can express an entire story and convince people in an emotionally powerful, morally compelling and rationally undeniable way.

---

5   These broadly correspond to the three modes of persuasion that Aristotle presents in *On Rhetorics: Logos, Ethos and Pathos.* Although in Rhetorics the mode Ethos is used to refer to the moral standing of the author or presenter, here we are using it to refer to the audience's moral sense.

Elements of Visual Persuasion

*Information, design,
networks & technology*

Working with visual information

RIGHT:
Glasses from Auschwitz at the Auschwitz-Birkenau Memorial and Museum. Photograph by Katrina Leno, 2010.

All advocates and campaigners collect information that they can then use strategically to influence policy and public debate, expose wrong-doing, push for justice, monitor those in power and regulate public institutions. Our effective use and presentation of information depends on our ability to communicate it successfully. While words used at the right time and in the right way can make a point very effectively, very few things are as powerful as images.

This goes beyond the adage 'a picture is worth a thousand words'. The overwhelming superiority of images to other forms such as sound or text when it comes to our ability to learn and remember has been recognised for some time and this is called the Picture Superiority Effect.[1] In addition, images can convey abstract concepts and use symbols to imply more complex ideas. The way we interact with images makes them especially useful when presenting information, and it is the framing of these images, their context and their packaging, that determines their communicative power in the context of campaigning. The image above, showing a pile of tangled spectacle frames, is taken from the Auschwitz museum. It portrays a certain fact, namely the large number of personal possessions that were broken and left behind at the camp. That is what we see, but this is not the full extent of the **information** being conveyed to us in this picture. Once we know where the image is from, what is brought to the fore is the magnitude of the tragedy; the pile of glasses mirrors the fate of those who once wore them.

---

1   This phenomenon is used in psychology, advertising and interface design.

This representation documents events differently from the way a list of statistics or names would do. It presents the facts of genocide, with the glasses taking on the force of evidence. Strictly speaking, however, this image is not actually evidence of a human tragedy, despite powerfully conveying a sense of horror. Rather, the image of a pile of glasses becomes an analogy for something that may be too painful to look at directly: the piles of bodies of people killed that we know existed at the camps.[2] Using this image to represent the tragedy can be more powerful, serving to evoke a much stronger image in the minds-eye. The image uses a specific, necessary and personal item to represent the whole story of the countless individuals who were killed. The image's persuasive power lies in the way it forces the viewer to fill in the details themselves, drawing on knowledge from history and popular culture. It does

not rely just on the image, but also on what the viewer already knows and brings to their reading of it. In contrast, the second image, also showing glasses (originally from the Buchenwald concentration camp this time), does not pretend to let the facts speak for themselves. The artist's intervention is clearly evident in this example. The glasses in this image belonged to 12 of the approximately 58,000 people who were murdered in Buchenwald by the Nazis during the Second World War. What this picture emphasises is the individuality of objects that in the previous image can be seen only as an anonymous mass. Their arrangement in this photograph is neither accidental nor decorative. What is interesting about this configuration is that the image is presented to the viewer as if it were indeed evidence. Side by side on a white background, the spectacles resemble evidence in a police investigation exhibit.

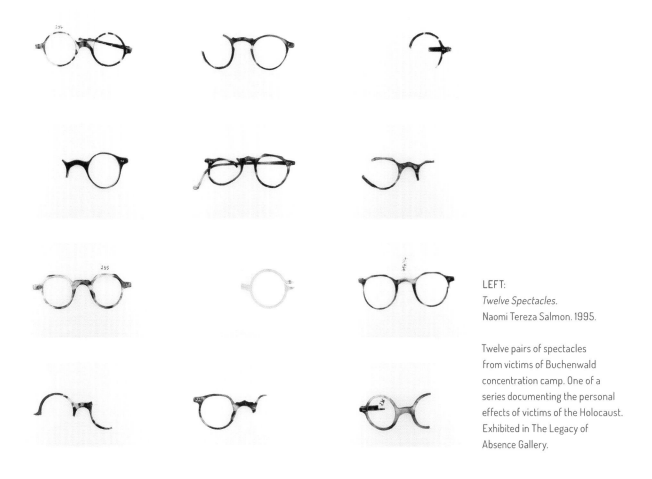

LEFT:
Twelve Spectacles.
Naomi Tereza Salmon. 1995.

Twelve pairs of spectacles from victims of Buchenwald concentration camp. One of a series documenting the personal effects of victims of the Holocaust. Exhibited in The Legacy of Absence Gallery.

2   The context in which an image is presented is significant here. For example, we may have a slightly higher tolerance for consuming such images in the news media, as they are understood as a report on current events. This is different to our reaction when such images are used to send a message to manipulate us. Because of this, the perceived authority of the creator of any visual information is also significant.

Although both of the images attempt to convey evidence, they must also be understood as careful representations of information. Often we think of visual information as being simply a fusion of words and/or numbers, laid out in a visual form; for example, an information graphic or map. But when we design visual campaigns, it is important also to understand images themselves as conveyors of information – from the information carried by the artefacts pictured to the implications of the framing and stylistic choices made by the creator of the campaign.

The way that the information is communicated is directly related to the form used to convey it; this is what we call its **design**. When we think about design, we tend to get caught up in ideas of taste, but good design in campaigns is design that engages people, using the aesthetic language of its audience and presenting visual information in a compelling way.

At first glance, the images in this series of campaign posters about freedom of expression online do not present information directly, as in the schematic of the *Brookes* or the photographs of glasses. Instead, they use a visual form to represent underlying facts. These images are not evidence for these facts; they refer to and convey information about repression. This indicates a significant difference in the intentions of the people who made these

images. In the previous example of the glasses, the use of metaphor softened the blow of what the image represents. Here, it is humour that tempers the seriousness of the message. We recognise the spoof dictators immediately through their distinct clothing and their opulent surroundings, which represent the trappings of power. The images remind us of the elephant's fear of the mouse, yet they also allude to the brutal and disproportionate violence that the dictators represented unleash as a reaction to this fear.

Understanding the difference between the information conveyed and the way it is framed in each of these examples can help us to understand the difference between the presentation of visual facts and the purposeful representation of ideas. In the first image of the glasses, the intention is to show the image as documentation and direct presentation of a fact. In the second image of the glasses, specific choices have been made by the artist, who has decided how to represent the glasses in order to direct the viewer's interpretation of the image. By contrast, the images of the dictators do not pretend to be presentations of evidence, but instead represent the perversity of repression through exaggeration and humour.

The two forms of representation used here, evidence and parody, are just two of the functions of visual information that we will explore in this guide. In the context of campaigning, we can judge the efficiency of a design by its capacity to:

▶ **Engage and entice:** its ability to get attention, often through an arresting or memorable image that presents a different perspective,

▶ **Communicate a convincing argument:** summarising complex concepts and communicating them through an aesthetic that the intended audience will respond to,

▶ **Draw the viewer in:** giving them a way to connect directly to the content or explore the issue further.

We will explore each of these elements in turn in the chapters of this book devoted to examples: *Get the Idea*, *Get the Picture* and *Get the Detail*.

LEFT:
Scared Leaders. International Society for Human Rights, 2010.
The International Society for Human Rights, working with the advertising agency Ogilvy and Mather, created a collection of posters on freedom of expression. The posters show the threat to different dictators posed by cyber-dissidents.

Putting visual information into action

Ultimately, a good design for visualising information for advocacy is one that achieves its intended purpose within a **network** of cultural, social and political interactions. In using visual information for advocacy, we have to consider its base of interaction, broadly to mean the network of people who engage with the issue in different ways. In order to create the schematic of the *Brookes*, the Abolitionists' access to the Quaker network was essential to help get information about the number of slaves on board. Similarly, they depended on a network of supporters to turn that information into posters. The ways in which information can be procured and deployed through a network are also affected by the use of and access to **technology**. This is still the case today, as it was at the time of the image of the *Brookes*, when the Abolitionists used the technologies

of the printing press, the archival system of the Liverpool customs house and the mail-coach and road systems for their communication.

Digital technologies are very important in this context because they provide new ways of accessing and sharing information. It is impossible to separate the way that people and their networks acquire and use information from the technologies that they use to do so. The ubiquity and ever-increasing accessibility of digital technologies have not only introduced new devices, tools and platforms for collecting, manipulating and sharing visual information, they have also inspired a movement of technologists, researchers and activists who are transforming the way we use technology to obtain and distribute visual information.

The possibilities of digital technologies have been seized upon by activists and citizens who find themselves becoming documentarists, archivists and monitors of abuses of power. Over the past few years, we have seen a revolution in public documentation, enabled by access to video cameras in mobile phones and by the prominence of video-sharing sites such as YouTube. This was demonstrated in 2010 when a YouTube video, aired on Al Jazeera and passed around social networks, became the defining event that set off the uprisings in Tunisia. The video showed the peaceful protest of the mother of a street vendor who had set himself on fire out of despair[3]. Video witnessing has the potential to trigger debate and transform public opinions into political engagement.

Videos, photographs and other forms of visual information, such as cartoons, have also been central to the emergence of networks of public witnesses. From Egypt to the United States and from Spain to Bahrain, citizens, journalists and activists are capturing visual evidence of police brutality, and sharing it on the internet. This has become a significant phenomenon, with blogs,

---

3   This man was Mohamed Bouazizi, a street vendor who set himself on fire after being harassed by municipal officials.

4   This has become a major issue in the US where the practice of filming the police is under debate: some of the more active online repositories are www.facebook.com/filmingcops, www.policemisconduct.net, www.policebrutality.info and http://copwatch.com

Facebook pages, websites and newsfeeds dedicated to the aggregation of such material.[4] Visual documentation is particularly powerful in aggregate, but it is only effective when it is used in the context of a network that can take advantage of the content. These networks extend from the people sharing, viewing and mobilising in response to the documentation to the police departments who are having to account for the behaviour of their officers.

This surge in visual public witnessing is a significant development. However, it is important to recognise that because of the flood of visual evidence that is emerging, issues of authenticity, verification and of scale are becoming more and more challenging.[5] This has already diminished the potential impact of such visual information in the context of advocacy and simultaneously shifts the burden of proof to the viewer who has to make a judgement call about the authenticity of the information they are looking at.

Other advances in digital technologies and the networks that emerge through them have also played a role in enabling activists to turn visual information into action. Google Maps and Google Earth have opened up cartography and taken it away from the dominance of the state and the military, de-monopolising the use of maps.[6] They have made it possible for anyone to create and mark up maps, and provided access to good-quality satellite imagery. Activists have taken advantage of these technologies and used them to gather and present information on a range

of issues, from drawing attention to the misuse of land in Bahrain to tagging undocumented prisons in Tunisia.[7] Alongside these developments, significant steps have been taken towards opening up the base data needed for mapping, thus enabling activists and journalists working in a wide range of contexts to reuse these mapping formats more extensively to deliver visual information. In turn, this has enabled the development of platforms such as Ushahidi[8], a tool aimed at civil society to enable crowd-mapping of events.

These four elements, **information**, **design**, **technologies** and **networks** are four elements that should be considered in every visual campaign. Whether we are presenting a narrative of genocide, inviting reflection on freedom of expression or documenting police violence, the quality of each of these elements will determine the effectiveness and reach of our campaign. It's important to learn to combine these factors: to know how best to use the available **technology**, in order to deliver the necessary **information** in its appropriate form or **design**, to the relevant **networks** of people. This combination will determine the **communicative power** of the images we create and, ultimately, the effectiveness of our campaigns. Of course, this is not a science but an art. Nonetheless, it is possible both to learn the techniques and to become more sensitive to what works and what doesn't.

ABOVE:

Journalists in Malaysia being attacked by police. Photograph published on Dr Dzul's blog, 2012.

LEFT:

Facebook You. Michel Kichka. 2011.

An increasing number of online collections bring together visual evidence to document police violence. This cartoon is one of the many images posted on the Facebook page, 'Filming Cops'.

5   Many human rights organisations are now integrating photographic and video documentation into larger and more systemic efforts to document atrocities. One such example can be found in this overview of air strikes on civilians in Syria, by Human Rights Watch. http://www.hrw.org/sites/default/files/reports/syria0413webwcover_1.pdf

6   Note that while these Google tools allow us to create our own maps, the actual basic data is not in the public domain and the maps we create are stored on Google's servers. Despite the freedoms they allow, none of the maps created using these tools are owned by their creators.

7   For more examples, see this post on Mapping as Campaigning: http://storify.com/hunginternet/mapping-as-campaigning-1

8   www.ushahidi.com

Forms of Influence

*Interruption,
education & coercion*

{ The success of an advocacy communication or campaign is shaped by its communicative power, but external factors such as political or social events, timing – even the weather – can affect it too. The purpose of this chapter is to bring together the concepts that we have discussed so far and to consider how to use and combine them in order to develop strategies for influencing people. What is the appropriate form of appeal – **rational**, **moral** or **emotional**? What is the best way to use and balance the four fundamental factors of communication – the content of the **information**, the **design** and its form, the **networks** of distribution and the **technology** employed?

Getting people to care; appealing to their values

The aim of activism is to change things from how they are to how they ought to be. Activists and their campaigns or advocacy efforts are in the business of asserting that the present situation is bad in some way, and that a particular possible future would be better. The present must be changed and something that is not now the case must become the case. In the middle of this movement between the present and the future hides the most important question, one that activists and campaigners must answer: **why**? *The answer to this question is the justification for the campaign.* It is critically important that we understand the reasons and arguments for our campaign's goal, or the change that we desire, because in one way or another, the campaign will have to express these reasons and stand behind them.

Activists often think that they can move their audience by issuing demands such as "Save the whales!" or "Free Nelson Mandela!". But such demands are seldom effective, because they try to force the hand of the audience. In order for them to work, the audience must already accept the justification for the demand and care about it.

Commitment to an issue is an expression of **care**. For an action to take place, somebody has to care sufficiently to want to change things **as they are** into things as they **ought to be**. People care in different ways: they care whether they are right or wrong, care about having the right and sufficient reasons to act, or they care because of an emotional commitment to something or someone. This emotional commitment is the strongest form of care, and normally has to do with proximity or connection. For example, someone might care more for their own dog than for a homeless person living in another part of the city, or they may care more about a country on the other side of the world, where a close relative lives, than for a neighbouring country. Since campaigning, or influencing people politically, is about getting them to care enough to prompt a change in the world, the real aim is to find a way to get people to extend their care. For example, to mobilise them to care about animals in general, or about countries where other people's relatives live. In this sense, *influence can be understood as the ability of a campaign to harness care*. Whether the audience is made up of policy makers, corporate executives or a community, the campaign has to generate enough care in these people to lead to a shift in opinions or a move to action.

The efficiency of an advocacy effort or campaign often depends not only on individuals but on generating the support of many or building critical mass. In campaigning terms, we often talk about this as solidarity or mobilisation, but it is helpful to recognise that essentially we are trying to develop communities that care about something.

If we want to persuade an audience to care about something and prompt change, we have to make an **appeal to their values**. Sometimes a campaign needs to show that values that people already share are being violated, and in certain other cases it must persuade people to apply their existing values to new issues. But just as often, the aim of a campaign is to instil new values or to change old ones. In any case, it is essential for the campaigner to know the audience and its current position: what are the values and beliefs that members of this audience already share? These can be recruited and appealed to in a campaign. What are the values and beliefs that are not shared? These must somehow be developed or instilled in the audience – a much more difficult undertaking.

In visual campaigns, a significant part of the job of expressing how things are, how they ought to be and why people should care **falls on the image**. Whether directly presented or implied, in any good visual campaign you should be able to read a visual argument: the facts of the matter and the problem, the implied promise of the future and the implied justification for change.

Getting it right

Certain things become clearer when we think of activism as moving something from its current deficient state to a brighter future, the most important of which may be that activism is not an end in itself. Keeping one eye on this promised future and the other on the shifting environment in which a campaign is operating is critical to success; as audiences respond, positions shift and events take new turns we have to be flexible, responsive and able to change direction. We need to know the audience and have a good grasp of the level of influence we can realistically expect to have, and it is essential to keep sight of a feasible goal if we are to track the efficiency of a campaign: if we know the desired result for a specific group, then there is a way to measure our success.

Knowing our audience and understanding how we will get them to care is critical in deciding how to formulate a strategy for using the four factors of communication – information, design, network and technologies – outlined in the previous chapter. This understanding can help us to decide what is the appropriate information, which is the right format, which networks we want to activate and what are the right technologies to use to to collect, shape and distribute the campaign. It is easy to see how important this is when we look at some of the things that could go wrong:

▶ Visual information aimed at people who are not ready to receive it or don't share our understanding of the problem can make the information useless; in this case we could be 'scratching where it doesn't itch'.[1]
▶ An image that people cannot bear to look at because it is too strong, such as explicit documentation of a tragedy, will not enlist support and, worse, may be perceived as manipulation.
▶ A campaign that makes use of the wrong technology platform for its particular audience will not reach it.

1   Eduardo Galeano's The Function of Art 2, from The Book of Embraces, W.W. Norton & Co. NY, London, 1989.

In all these ways, a good campaign is like a good joke. A joke's effectiveness lies in the choice of the right words, good timing, a convincing delivery and a funny punch-line. A good joke is memorable and is easily shared and passed between people. All of these factors ultimately depend on having an understanding of the values and beliefs of the audience and on the authority of the person delivering the joke. A large part of a campaign's effectiveness can depend on finding an affinity between the people delivering it and the people receiving it.

"Black Cloud"

While the Chinese economy is booming, the skies above its cities are darkening. One of the biggest causes is the phenomenal growth in the number of cars and exhaust emissions. To kick off their '20 tips for sustainable development' campaign and drive people to their 20to20.org mini-site, WWF expressed one tip in dramatic fashion. Along with an increase in new volunteers, WWF received coverage of the event in a number of Chinese newspapers as well as on CCTV 9, Beijing TV, Phoenix TV; even international news stations as far away as Deutsche Welle Broadcasting in Germany and Al Jazeera in the Middle East.

On balloon:
Drive one day less and look how much carbon monoxide you'll keep out of the air we breathe.

Strategies of intervention

There are many strategies for intervening in an issue; broadly speaking they can be divided into three categories with some variation and overlap:

▶ **Interruption:** *questioning* the dominant narrative, disrupting its usual meaning.

▶ **Education:** *shifting* the dominant narrative and transforming the way people understand a particular issue.

▶ **Coercion:** compelling action by some type of force or threat of force, which usually involves *challenging* the dominant narrative to reveal concealed facts.

Before we examine these approaches, it may be useful to note that digital technologies and increased access to information have made it easier to use strategies of interruption, education and coercion. These advances are important not only because they democratise the sharing of and access to information but also because they permit interventions over long distances and across social, cultural and political borders. Technology has had a particularly strong impact on interventions that seek to connect problems that emerge in one place but are rooted in another, such as pollution or resource extraction. This is something we will see through the case studies in the following chapters.

▶ INTERRUPTION

Interruption works to challenge the dominant narrative or jar the normal way of seeing things. It can build on the way people already care about things, but it can also act as a reminder or invitation to like-minded people, calling them to put their care into action. Interruption can be used to disrupt people's existing patterns of caring, encouraging them to ask questions about their own commitments and unthinking assumptions.

Black Cloud, a project created by the World Wildlife Fund in China, attempts to question some of these 'unthought' patterns of care by using a striking visual device to convey a message about the rapid growth in the number of cars in China and therefore in the amount of exhaust emissions. The World Wildlife Fund attached a cloud-shaped balloon to the exhaust-pipe of a car. The balloon fills up as the car is driven, creating an inflated black cloud with the words: "Look how much carbon monoxide you'll keep out of the air we breathe by not driving for just one day" written on it. The balloon not only interrupts the line of sight of passers-by, it also disrupts their understanding of the car and the air around it. The entirely opaque bubble contains the fumes that would otherwise quickly disappear into thin air. This, of course, is not a presentation of documented evidence; instead, the bubble is used to emphasise an aspect of pollution, making visible something that is normally invisible. Its form, and its irruption in the everyday street scene, shift our perception of the cars in the street and force us to question whether or not we care enough to abstain from using our own cars.

LEFT:
Black Cloud. World Wildlife Fund and Ogilvy Beijing, China. 2007.

LEFT:
Playing cards from *La Baraja Popular*, a 48-card pack, issued at the time of Perón's election campaign. Argentina, 1951.

LEFT:
Anti-Peronist cards.
Juan José Ruiz.

These sets of playing cards from Argentina are an example of an interruption that uses dominant narrative to create counter-narrative. The first set of cards was circulated in Argentina in 1951 to celebrate the Perón regime and promote Perón in the upcoming election campaign. The cards show the Perón regime as 'saviours of the people'. Perón looks almost like a movie star with his slick hair and white dinner jacket, and the symbols that surround him reinforce his claims offering protection, security and safety. The second set of cards, released anonymously, was a direct response to the official set. The anti-Peronist deck uses storytelling to construct a counter-narrative that exposes the dark side of the leader and his administration. The 12 of Batons, for example, shows Perón in his military attire portrayed as a thief, a greedy and crooked leader. The Ace of Cups shows military personnel hoarding money and property that was intended for homeless victims of the 1944 San Juan earthquake.

The anti-Peronist playing cards, work as a form of visual information, one that has the effect of interrupting the status quo and creating bonds between like-minded people. The cards use wit to make an appeal to the intellect, humour to soften the heaviness of the content, and symbolic references (needing to be decoded by the user) to appeal to a sense of reason. The references alluding to specific details of broader political events need to be decoded and therefore foster 'insider' cohesion among those who own and play with the cards. In a way, this is similar to what we can imagine happening with the china cups produced by the Abolitionists.

Interruptions such as this one can help break the dominant narrative, however mostly such interventions are effective in aggregate. However, while one artfully executed single interruption in the right place at the right time can have a big impact on an audience, mostly such interventions are effective in aggregate. Taking the long view on such interruptions can help us to have more realistic expectations about the impact each intervention of this sort can have; it contributes to a counter-narrative, stacks up and serves to create bonds within a community, and it nudges those who are sitting on the fence. It is important to recognise that such interventions may seem clever, but mostly appeal to the like-minded, and are often easily dismissed by those who have an opposing view or a pre-existing allegiance to an opposing group.

▶ EDUCATION

Educational interventions often do deeper work, transforming people's perceptions over time by gradually shifting the dominant narrative and thus bringing us to new answers; for example, making us look afresh at the conduct of the financial industry or, redefining our understanding of banking.

As they tend to call for larger shifts in perception, educational interventions are often protracted and involve actions by many groups, or interconnected campaigns over a long period. The educational approach to campaigning is most effective when it takes a slow-burn or indirect approach and when the audience is not directly aware that it is 'being campaigned at'. This is why popular culture forms such as television and film are particularly significant in bringing about these changes. Although films can be very helpful in changing attitudes, the cost involved means they

remain somewhat under-exploited as a campaigning tool.[2]

However, single campaigns that work over time to change people's minds about an issue can still be effective, as we have seen with the success of organisations such as Greenpeace, whose systematic and widespread long-term visual campaigns have changed our perception of the environment.

The Lebanese campaign, *Khede Kasra*[3], is an example of an educational intervention that used visual information in an attempt to shift the discussion around a long-term and complex set of issues related to gender equality in Lebanon. Instead of addressing these issues directly, the Women Empowerment Program at the Hariri Foundation worked with advertising agency Leo Burnett to create a campaign that would draw people's attention to how, at the level of fundamental daily practice, the Arabic language

2   See Jeff Skoll's venture, Participant Media, for an example of a production house dedicated to changing meanings and campaigning through mainstream films: http://www.participantmedia.com/

3   http://www.pewforum.org/2013/07/16/gay-marriage-around-the-world-2013/#spain

4   https://en.wikipedia.org/wiki/Gay_marriage_in_Spain

excludes women. The campaign focused on the use of language, and in particular on the accent (Kasra) that in Arabic is placed underneath a word to make it clear that a word is feminine or addressed to a woman – as opposed to being above the word to make it clear it is addressed to a male, or omitted, in which case the word is masculine by default. The campaign shows this mark in red, placing it underneath words written in black, choosing words for the posters and adverts that would take on a different meaning when the accent was added. The campaign was rolled out on billboards, and in magazines with stickers attached so that people could add the red accent themselves, where they wanted it (see image, right). This campaign was then extended beyond posters and magazines, producing red 'accent' pins worn, for example, by television presenters (see image, left). These pins were catalysts for debates and discussions. The use of the accent and the fundamental question of gendered language was a simple way to start a dialogue about equality, and it was its wide-spread exposure and the diversity of those who carried it forward – from female celebrities to male television presenters – that contributed to its success.

An educational intervention like the *Khede Kasra* campaign can be seen as just a stepping stone, laying the foundations for a much larger challenge and working in combination with other campaigns over time to try to shift the dominant perception – in this case, of women's rights, while campaigning in parallel for concrete policy changes that address the imbalances.

It is very difficult to force communities into fundamental cultural shifts just by changing policies from above, especially where there is either a single dominant opposing trend or pockets of strong opposition. Therefore change that comes from above or is implemented by force in the way of legal measures may need to be supported by other efforts, such as educational interventions. Gay marriage is a clear case in point. Advocates in Spain, for example, were successful in obtaining the legalisation, in 2005, of gay marriage. However, after this policy change, many people in Spain asked for a repeal of the Law as a considerable part of the population had not yet come along with the change.[4] To be persuaded to support gay marriage, the audience must already have a strong 'instinctive' belief in the ideas of equality and rights – not just when the legislation is enacted, but also afterwards, while the changes are being implemented.

LEFT & RIGHT:
Khede Kasra campaign Hariri
Foundation and Leo Burnett
Beirut, 2009.

▶ COERCION

Coercion in campaigning aims mainly to influence the people who directly oppose a position or will not change in response to other kinds of appeal. It leads audiences to look behind the dominant narrative, at the details. When it is not possible to influence opponents to reconsider their position or shift their understanding of an issue, many campaigns resort to threatening the relevant actor/s in order to compel them to action. Making a specific and public accusation or exposing wrong-doing can, in some circumstances, be effective. This is especially the case if time is short. Coercion uses different types of threats, such as public shame, financial or legal repercussions. This can be a risky approach. Such tactics can make it difficult to maintain control of a campaign. In such situations, the emphasis is on timing and responsiveness, opportunism, the formation of strategic alliances, flexibility and access to sufficient resources.

In 2009, a scandal exploded around the expenses claimed by British Members of Parliament (MPs). The path towards this revelation had initially been made by journalists and freedom of information campaigners requesting disclosure of information on specifically named MPs' expenses under the Freedom of Information Act. The Guardian Datablog created an infographic poster highlighting specific aspects of the scandal and allowed readers to download a spreadsheet that contained the specific details of each of the categories of expense claims. This spreadsheet enabled users to go through all of the information and explore, line by line, the ways in which many individuals among the more than 600 MPs broke the law and abused their position for personal gain. The data was organised by parliament member and constituency, along with exact details of what was claimed.

By making the data available as a spreadsheet – a choice of format that served to present the details as facts – The Guardian made specific information about misconduct available directly, empowering members of the public to analyse the records of their own MPs. The data produced by campaigning organisations and by activists was widely amplified by the media, leading to a major political scandal and ultimately forcing a number of MPs to repay expenses that they had wrongly claimed. Some MPs, including the Speaker of the House, resigned from their posts, and criminal charges were brought against three others. This is an example of exposure at work.

ABOVE:
A year in expenses.
The Guardian. 5 February 2010.

BELOW:
MPs Expenses Claimed 2008/09.
Spreadsheet available on The Guardian's datablog.
Data organised by parliament member, constituency and exact details of what was claimed.

iament yesterday released the full details of MPs' claims for 2008-09. This is a snapshot

Smallest repayment

40p

Labour's Mike Gapes, MP for Ilford South was asked to pay this after Sir Paul Kennedy ruled that he was entitled to claim a council tax payment after all

Average total claim, by MP

Conservative	£139,460
Labour	£151,140
LibDem	£158,000

Totals are dominated by geography. MPs from Scotland - including many Liberal Democrats representing far northern constituencies will have higher travel costs, for instance

Strange paybacks

£180

paid back by Shahid Malik, MP for Dewsbury, for a massage chair. Meanwhile Clare Short had to pay back £3,188, including excessive claims for gardening and a £1,206 mobile phone claim against her second home allowance

Big lunches

6,777

guests were entertained in the House of Commons by Keith Vaz, MP for Leicester East, who hosted 58 events there. The most events were hosted by Evan Harris, Lib Dem MP for Oxford West and Abingdon - 89

Who repaid the most?

Barbara Follett *Stevenage*	£42,458.21
Bernard Jenkin *North Essex*	£36,909.17
Andrew Mackay *Bracknell*	£31,193.00
David Heathcoat-Amory *Wells*	£29,691.93
John Gummer *Suffolk Coastal*	£29,398.46
Julie Kirkbride *Bromsgrove*	£29,243.00
Jonathan Djanogly *Huntingdon*	£25,000.00
Liam Fox *Woodspring*	£24,878.27
Paul Goggins *Wythenshawe*	£21,307.15
Douglas Hogg *Sleaford & North Hykeham*	£20,639.42

Does not include Phil Hope, who repaid more than was recommended

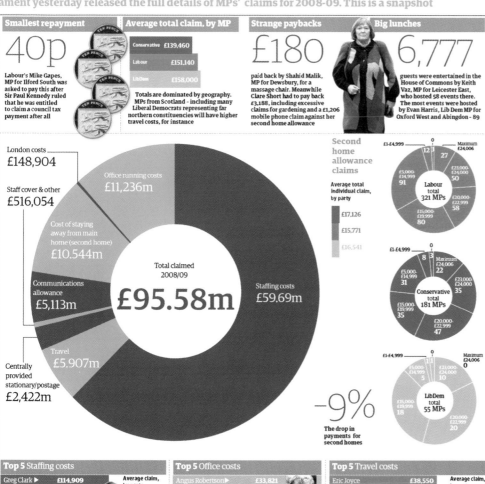

London costs £148,904

Staff cover & other £516,054

Cost of staying away from main home (second home) £10.544m

Communications allowance £5,113m

Travel £5.907m

Centrally provided stationary/postage £2,422m

Office running costs £11,236m

Total claimed 2008/09

£95.58m

Staffing costs £59.69m

Second home allowance claims

Average total individual claim, by party

- £17,126
- £15,771
- £16,541

Labour total 321 MPs

- £1-£4,999: 12
- £5,000-£14,999: 91
- £15,000-£19,999: 80
- £20,000-£22,999: 58
- £23,000-£24,000: 50
- Maximum £24,006: 27
- 0: 3

Conservative total 181 MPs

- £1-£4,999: 8
- £5,000-£14,999: 31
- £15,000-£19,999: 35
- £20,000-£22,999: 47
- £23,000-£24,000: 35
- Maximum £24,006: 22
- 0: 3

LibDem total 55 MPs

- £1-£4,999: 1
- £5,000-£14,999: 5
- £15,000-£19,999: 18
- £20,000-£23,999: 20
- £23,000-£24,000: 10
- Maximum £24,006: 0
- 0: 1

-9%

The drop in payments for second homes

Totals repaid by party

£598,153 | £427,152 | £427,745

£4,227 Average individual Conservative repayment

£3,237 Average individual Labour repayment

£1,910 Average individual Lib Dem repayment

Top 5 Staffing costs

Greg Clark ▶ *Tunbridge Wells*	£114,909
Roger Godsiff *B'ham Sparkbrook & Small Heath*	£113,729
Nick Herbert *Arundel & South Downs*	£112,456
Margaret Beckett *Derby South*	£112,213
Stephen Pound *Ealing North*	£111,938

Average claim, by party
£88,841 | £94,159 | £94,253

Top 5 Office costs

Angus Robertson ▶ *Moray*	£33,821
Bridget Prentice ▶ *Lewisham East*	£31,982
Dave Watts *St Helens North*	£31,968
Evan Harris *Oxford West and Abingdon*	£31,066
Helen Jones *Warrington North*	£30,218

Top 5 Travel costs

Eric Joyce *Falkirk*	£38,550
Alistair Carmichael *Orkney and Shetland*	£35,472
Charles Kennedy *Ross, Skye & Lochaber*	£35,260
John Thurso *Caithness, Sutherland and Easter Ross*	£34,405
Danny Alexander *Inverness, Nairn, Badenoch and Strathspey*	£32,949

Average claim, by party
£6,897 | £9,770 | £10,842

Cost of ng away om main me (2nd home)	London costs	Office running costs	Staffing costs	Travel	Centrally provided stationary	Staff cover & other	Comms allowance	TOTAL CLAIMED, 08/09	TOTAL CLAIMED 07/08	% change, 07/08 to 08/09	2nd home allowance claim 2007/08	% change in second home claime, 07/08 to 08/09
18,582	0	11,951	108,264	1,387	6,972	0	8,748	156,405	153,138	2	20,766	-11
23,640	0	24,251	97,530	14,558	2,062	0	10,300	172,341	167,561	3	22,905	3
19,359	0	10,594	88,858	8,115	3,845	0	9,467	140,239	141,625	-1	20,486	-5
23,301	0	22,129	86,619	6,600	2,317	0	15,406	156,372	145,585	8	20,721	12
24,006	0	20,321	78,467	9,977	6,906	0	10,484	150,161	160,542	-7	23,083	4
21,995	0	23,555	97,938	24,352	853	0	2,711	171,403	117,268	34	17,312	27
0	0	20,250	88,578	8,174	2,784	0	10,371	130,157	132,218	-2	0	0
16,855	0	20,795	93,360	18,946	4,740	0	6,045	160,741	156,932	3	14,557	16
10,045	0	12,166	68,579	5,779	698	0	4,047	101,314	96,202	3	9,530	5
22,404	0	14,139	74,750	3,905	3,944	0	0	119,142	121,352	-2	20,194	11
21,521	0	5,489	59,702	6,018	2,758	0	0	95,488	89,133	5	14,918	44
16,762	0	19,001	94,963	4,730	962	0	8,129	144,546	136,199	9	21,631	-23
19,900	0	23,364	97,871	24,079	4,808	0	6,784	178,804	167,846	8	21,737	-8
11,363	0	12,293	109,530	5,348	5,084	0	8,714	152,332	144,984	4	17,976	-37
21,785	0	18,167	95,214	15,269	5,473	0	13,769	169,678	158,136	8	23,041	-5
21,417	0	25,708	94,102	5,196	2,783	12,423	3,506	165,135	152,822	8	23,083	-7
23,988	0	23,200	98,359	23,119	2,588	0	10,489	181,743	169,427	8	23,083	4
16,079	0	13,884	76,695	9,058	4,648	0	153	120,518	125,602	-3	16,162	-1
12,770	0	19,673	95,867	8,081	2,320	0	3,935	142,646	154,625	-10	23,083	-45
24,006	0	12,540	90,191	7,183	2,359	0	12,707	148,986	154,848	-4	22,573	6
15,418	0	13,968	90,622	6,759	3,527	0	6,430	136,725	142,848	-4	17,892	-14

Travel	Centrally provided stationary	Staff cover & other	Comms allowance	TOTAL CLAIMED, 08/09
1,887	6,972	0	8,748	156,405
14,558	2,062	0	10,300	172,341
8,115	3,845	0	9,467	140,239
6,600	2,317	0	15,406	156,372
9,977	6,906	0	10,484	150,161
24,352	853	0	2,711	171,403
8,174	2,784	0	10,371	130,157
18,946	4,740	0	6,045	160,741
5,779	698	0	4,047	101,314
3,905	3,944	0	0	119,142
6,018	2,758	0	0	95,488
4,730	962	0	8,129	144,546

In another example we can see a different intervention at work in the form of monitoring. *The Land Matrix* is the project of a coalition of organisations, documenting land acquisition deals globally. Tactical Tech worked to make the data collected by these groups public. Several groups had different sets of data, going back as far as the 1980s and ranging from newspaper articles about land deals to actual copies of contracts. This data was eventually merged across the organisations to create the world's largest database of land acquisition deals, holding information on over two thousand transactions. Tactical Tech worked with the coalition to decide how to present the data and make it accessible to different audiences. We decided to make one thousand of the most verifiable records available to the public, using visualisation to allow users to explore the database from different perspectives, including which countries were buying the most land and who was buying from whom. While the coalition was aware that their decision to track this information was in itself already

setting an agenda and defining a specific problem, they made a strategic decision to avoid overt campaigning in order to preserve, as much as possible, their reputations as unbiased researchers. For this reason, they took an open-source approach to the data, making it available for direct download and reuse with the hope of providing grassroots activists and investigative journalists with information that could be used in many different ways. When the online visualisations and database platforms were launched, there was an overwhelming response, with visits to the coalition's website jumping tenfold from 3,000 to 30,000 per month. The coverage they received went beyond exposure based on press releases and resulted in journalists making their own stories out of the content of the Land Matrix, and in activists from specific countries using the data to formulate campaigns.

ABOVE:

The Land Matrix. The Land Coalition in partnership with Tactical Tech, 2012.

Combining interventions

Strategies for intervention are often combined. Choosing which kind of intervention to emphasise for which audience is very important when we plan a visual information campaign. This decision is largely driven by the situation and the context.

For example, in the case of imminent ethnic violence an educational intervention will not work quickly enough, so interruption or coercion may be better strategies. In the case of long-standing tensions between two communities or countries, however, an educational intervention may have more potential to alleviate the conflict in the long run. By contrast, in a case where persecution is fuelled by some people for political gain, coercion may be a risky, yet more effective, form of intervention.

However, it is important to remember that none of these three kinds of intervention ever exists in pure form. The choice of emphasis is a strategic question that may ultimately affect the outcome of a campaign. The right decision needs to be informed by a profound understanding of the problem we want to solve and of what the barriers to change are. We need to know who has the power to make this change and resolve the problem, and we need a realistic view of how to get those people to care and, ultimately, of what form of influence will work best.

 Through three in-depth case studies we can see how the elements examined so far, work in actual campaigns and how they exert influence by artfully combining different forms of appeal, different factors of communication and different types of intervention.

Plastic waste in the ocean

RIGHT:
Campaign poster by
Greenpeace with Publicis
Mojo Auckland. Photograph of
albatross chick, copyright David
Liittschwager, 2005. Photograph
of stomach contents, copyright
Susan Middleton, 2005.

HOW TO STARVE TO DEATH ON A FULL STOMACH. The 272 pieces of rubbish pictured
above were fed to this fledgling albatross along with fish caught by its mother. The plastic

Research shows that there is a thick layer of plastic waste three times the size of Spain floating on the surface of the ocean. But does that statement, in itself, resonate with you or have any impact on whether you care about the problem?

These pictures, above, were taken by two wildlife photographers, and later used by Greenpeace for a campaign. The photographers were documenting wildlife on the Kure Atoll in the Hawaiian archipelago, one of the remotest islands in the Pacific Ocean. The chick in the photograph lived near their equipment storage shed and they nicknamed it 'Shed Bird'. When they found the chick dead they investigated further and what they discovered

became the focus of the image that you now see in the poster. Albatrosses are surface feeders who survive on squid and fish eggs rather than diving for their food as many other seabirds do. Gyres, places where ocean currents converge, are their hunting grounds. In the past fifty years, these gyres have become choked with plastic debris, which the birds mistake for food, pick off of the surface and regurgitate into their chicks' hungry mouths. Shed Bird died because its stomach was full of plastic and no longer had the space to digest food.

Susan Middleton, one of the photographers, says about the issue of plastics in the ocean: "The problem with the

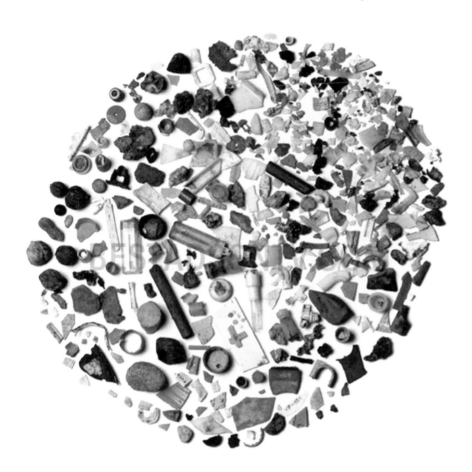

GREENPEACE

accumulated in its stomach until it was literally 'too full to eat'. Careless and unregulated dumping is
just one of the ways we're killing our oceans. Become an ocean defender at oceans.greenpeace.org

Pacific garbage patch is that I've never seen a picture of it that's compelling. When we go out there, they say there's garbage floating over an area the size of the state of Texas. So we sort of imagine it, then we want to see the pictorial evidence of it, and when we're actually out there, it's not like we're knee deep in garbage. There's a lot of it slightly subsurface, so the pictures don't convey it. However, that photograph of 13.8 ounces of mostly plastic inside the stomach of one bird tells the story."

The photographs were then picked up by Greenpeace and used in a campaign with the tagline "How to starve to death on a full stomach". The curated image makes a rational appeal by establishing a connection between the act of disposing of plastic and the pollution of the sea. It makes a moral claim on the audience's sense of duty towards the environment, but it also has a strong emotional appeal as the horror of a dead baby bird with a belly full of plastic sinks in. The picture invites viewers to probe their relationship with the floating objects and wonder how they were disposed of. Some of the objects are recognisable and may be used by the viewer every day – a lighter, a bottle top, a key chain – and the logical association puts the burden of responsibility on the viewer. The presentation of the stomach contents also raises troubling questions that it feels absurd to have to ask: how do 13.8 ounces of plastic fit into a baby bird? How does plastic find its way to a remote island in the Pacific Ocean, hundreds of miles from the nearest human settlement? Since the audience is eating from the same sea as the albatross, the image also points to the fact that ultimately the audience may be responsible for its own demise, which may mirror that of the bird. All of these questions that arise interrupt the sense that this has nothing to do with us. This leads us to reconsider our own actions and those of our neighbours, and to think about the need to correct the practices that contribute to this, such as the illegal dumping of waste.

This visual campaign uses the power of synecdoche, which we explored in the introduction. That is, a part of the problem is used to represent the whole problem. Middleton believes that it was the story of this one bird – the authorities performed necropsies on 55 other chicks and found that they had died in similar ways – that evoked a strong response: "We resonate with the plight of someone half a world away that we've heard about in the news, who is undergoing some kind of terrible suffering. That somehow emotes, or ignites more of a response in us than just statistics of hundreds of thousands of people suffering. Why is it that an individual resonates with us so much more strongly than hundreds of thousands? Because we don't really know them; then it becomes an abstraction, and it's not real. It's not one person, or one bird. I think that makes a difference in how effectively things are communicated."

These images, and the story of the chick itself, have been used in advocacy aimed at the United States government, and they have contributed to bringing about stronger environmental protection of this part of the Pacific Ocean. It is now the largest protected marine environment in the world. Middleton reports that the head of the White House Council on Environmental Quality at the time, Jim Connaughton, said to her, "Your book and your exhibition are the single most valuable tool that I have to persuade people on the Hill [the US Congress] to say that this area needs to be protected".

This visual campaign successfully used a blend of information and design with the clear purpose of influencing an audience that was targeted by both Greenpeace and the photographers. In making different appeals: rational, moral and emotional, the visual representation was more effective than a set of facts about how many birds die each year, or a direct slogan telling the audience what to think or do. Its communicative power lies in the representation of visual data as evidence and in pushing the viewer to do the work of filling in the logical connections that make up the argument. Its artfulness lies in its careful representation of the right story to convey the whole message while making a very strong emotional and ethical appeal, without underestimating the rational capacity of the audience.

Challenging Chevron

DESTROYING COMMUNITIES SHOULDN'T BE PROFITABLE, BUT IT IS!

WE AGREE.

Jamie Way
Community Organizer
Village Earth

John S. Watson
Chairman of the Board & CEO
Chevron

Thanks to a leak from a web advertising agency about a new advertising campaign by the multinational oil company Chevron, Rainforest Action Network, Amazon Watch and The Yes Men staged a hoax campaign. The campaign mimicked and mocked the original Chevron campaign that represented the company as an organisation working in the public interest with the bold and unifying statement 'We Agree'. The three NGOs collaborated, mobilising their networks to act on the leak, gaining access to the

ABOVE:

This image is a parody of a similar poster created by Chevron to promote its "corporate social responsibility" work. The image was submitted by an activist to the Chevron Thinks We're Stupid Campaign, 2010.
The parody contains pictures of real children affected by pollution from oil drilling in Ecuador that resulted in Chevron being ordered to pay USD 8.6 billion.

Energy shouldn't cost lives

THE PROBLEM | THE SOLUTION | GET INVOLVED | ABOUT | MEDIA

We Can CHANGE Chevron

Click on the faces below and select your board member!

ADOPT A CHEVRON BOARD MEMBER

Kevin W. Sharer

Kevin is the Chairman, CEO and President of the biotechnology company Amgen, Inc. He graduated from the US Naval Academy in 1970 and served until 1978. He received an MBA from University of Pittsburg. He also served on both the Bush and McCain National Election Committees.

Board Position

Management Compensation, Nominating & Governance Committees

Location

Thousand Oaks, California

Affiliations

ADOPT KEVIN »

Adopting a Chevron Board member is a fun and easy way to make a real difference. With your adoptive attention Chevron's Board members can help end the suffering caused by Chevron's oil contamination in Ecuador. Pick one Board member to focus on and help send a loud message to

advertising campaign design and plans in advance of the launch. The hoax campaign used the technique of imitating the genuine advertising campaign's design, and the Chevron slogan, 'We Agree', parodying Chevron. Their intervention not only mimicked the advertising campaign visually but also used loop-holes in the technologies of distribution to create further confusion; for example, creating a spoof online domain for the campaign, with the URL 'http://www.chevron-weagree.com/', so that journalists were not sure if they were looking at the real Chevron website or not.

On the day of the Chevron advertising campaign's launch, but just a few hours earlier, the NGO campaigners put out a fake press release, using language typical of such documents and making pro-environment claims on behalf of Chevron:

"Chevron is making a clean break from the past by taking direct responsibility for our own actions", said Rhonda Zygocki, Chevron vice president of Policy, Government and Public Affairs. "Oil Companies Should Clean Up Their Messes", reads one ad; the small print refers candidly to the damage done by oil companies around the world.

"For decades, oil companies like ours have worked in disadvantaged areas, influencing policy in order to do there what we can't do at home. It's time this changed."

Due to the trend for oil companies like Chevron to use greenwashing, many US media outlets were actually unable to tell if they were looking at the real press release and the real Chevron campaign or the fake ones. When Chevron did release their own campaign and statement later that day, the extent of the stunt became clear, with some journalists choosing to write a story about the hoax campaign rather than about Chevron's.[5]

The campaigners were successful because they had a strong understanding of the networks they could access and a strong design that mocked the company, using technology to do so. They used these factors to play the particular context they were working in, that of the company and the technology they would use to do so, they played well to the particular context they were working in, that of the US media environment. Ironically, they successfully managed to spin a system that is notorious for

5   http://www.reuters.com/article/2010/10/18/chevron-hoax-idAFN1827001220101018?sp=true

its own spin tactics. This campaign worked because of the nature of corporate communications. Not everyone has a target that is quite so easy to parody effectively. As David Taylor of the Rainforest Action Network says:

"Branding is very important to oil companies. They can spend several hundred million dollars over two or three years just on advertising and on their brand image; they spend a lot of money to brand themselves as 'good', and not as the 'worst' of all companies. They seek to create doubt in the public mind, that they are 'not as bad as' the next oil company, or that they compensate in some way." Rainforest Action Network took a huge risk in undertaking a confrontational campaign, using such an aggressive form of interruption. Yet part of the beauty of the campaign lies in their success in posing as the company and mocking a style of communication that many recognise as mere posturing and manipulation. The campaign took this one step further by creating a spoof web-page inviting people to 'Adopt a Chevron Board Member' (see image, left). Users could click on each of the board members' profiles and read about them and then opt to, for example, 'adopt Kevin'. This allowed them to write directly to Kevin about their concerns regarding Chevron. In creating an 'adopt a board member' page, the hoax campaign was also mimicking the language of development NGOs, which use mechanisms such as 'adopt a child' to get financial backing from supporters.

The use of humour in this highly provocative campaign softens the blow of the message, drawing people in. It is worth noting that the Yes Men, a group of activists known for their daring exposures of the corporate sector, operate as artists precisely because this gives them more room to stretch campaigns into events and practises that other people may find outrageous. Their status as artists gives the group greater protection from litigation. The Yes Men take a deliberately daring stance, knowing that if they are sued they will get even more media attention and, in turn, invite greater scrutiny of the misconduct of the companies they are campaigning against.

Rainforest Action Network justify this approach by explaining that they believe there is little or no room for negotiation, dialogue or mitigation when confronted with such a large and powerful corporation, and that any such techniques are just not effective.

"You can't really create a set of facts about oil dumping or drilling, or climate change, to make them change their behaviour. You can only paint them as bad guys, so that the public doesn't feel sympathetic to them or let them off the hook. Chevron Texaco has been found guilty and has been slapped with one of the largest financial liabilities for oil pollution ever. This means something, it has a huge impact in people's minds, but it doesn't mean necessarily that they have a desire to be a good corporate citizen. You want to create a public perception of them as such an evil actor till they deal with remediation and show that they have accountability."

Through this example, we can see that the way in which a visual campaign is rolled out is a significant part of an intervention. By taking advantage of the leak obtained by their network, carefully using information that substantiated their claims of Chevron's misconduct, designing a plausible hoax and taking advantage of technologies that reinforced this hoax, RAN brought the public's attention to the issue of oil company greenwashing. But even though the campaign was original, well-designed and loved by many who saw it for its daring and clever execution, it is important in the context of this guide to look at the question of its impact.

A campaign that uses parody speaks to the converted. In other words, this campaign had the most impact among those who already had some affinity with the hoaxers' position. This affinity was what made some viewers find the story of the unfolding hoax amusing rather than menacing or irreverent. The campaign was successful in that it attracted media attention and the support of people who already distrusted Chevron and other large oil companies. Yet it did not seem to have a significant effect on people who believe that oil companies do the best they can, such as investors in the companies and their principal stakeholders, including oil consumers. Nor did the campaign change the activities of Chevron. In fact, Chevron Texaco were still running their own unchanged advertising campaign, the same one that had been spoofed, in mainstream magazines two years after RAN's parody was released.

LEFT:
Adopt a Chevron Board Member screenshot from *We Can Change Chevron* campaign. Rainforest Action Network.

That's right...
An island! Look for the yacht...
And note the size of it...

A horse track

Land abuse in Bahrain

When the government ordered Internet Service Providers to block Google Earth and Google Video in Bahrain in 2006, it drew much more attention to what they blocked than if they had simply done nothing. Rumours that the reason for the block was a set of satellite images were quickly followed up with a PDF document that circulated around the internet by email and was posted to different websites.[6]

The 45-page document compiled screenshots from Google Earth and annotated them, allowing the audience to see satellite images of the large tracts of land and lavish palaces owned by the Royal family in this very small and densely-populated country. The images showed land used by the minority Sunni monarchy, detailing golf courses, islands, stables and palaces that were otherwise unknown to the public. For people who could no longer see the details on Google Earth, the PDF documented them and took advantage of digital technologies to circulate visual evidence showing the illegal and private distribution of 30% of Bahrain's total land area.

The hand of the author is barely evident in the selection and framing of the images grabbed from Google Earth, and they are powerful precisely because they purport to present the facts, as evidence of abuses of power. The images were taken from a resource – Google Earth – the aim of which is to provide accurate satellite images of earth. The fact that the service was then blocked lent credibility and drew attention to the "truth" of their contents. The sense of concealed inequality was greatly exacerbated by a senior government official, who made a statement to the press accusing Google Earth of having "... allowed the public to pry into private homes and ogle people's motor yachts and swimming pools".[7]

What happened next was driven by the on-line and off-line network of political and social conversations that emerged around the images, both locally – thanks to prominent bloggers such as Mahmood Yousif, through his political blog Mahmood's Den – and globally through networks of online activists and the mainstream media, who picked up the stories from bloggers and activists. Writing in the Financial Times, journalist William Wallis stated:

"Opposition activists claim that 80% of the island has been carved up between royals and other private landlords, while much of the rest of the population faces an acute housing shortage ... Some of the palaces take up more space than three or four villages nearby and block access to

6   http://www.ft.com/cms/s/0/d14d3576-7bfa-11db-b1c6-0000779e2340.html#axzz2UqLBbrtB
7   Financial Times, November 24, 2006.

A golf course...

It's the King's favourite property! It's the size of Malkiyya, Karzakkan, Sadad and Shahrakkan together!

the sea for fishermen. People knew this already. But they never saw it. All they saw were the surrounding walls", said Mr Yousif, who is seen in Bahrain as the grandfather of its blogging community."[8]

Given the context, it is easy to imagine how this cartography of inequality made clear the imbalance in land distribution and the disproportionate ownership of assets by the ruling class. The images make use of all three kinds of appeal: they reveal the truth about how this land was used, they evoke a sense of moral injustice; and for people who struggled to get enough land or adequate housing they ignited an emotional reaction of outrage.

Despite the wide circulation and exposure of the visual evidence, there was no direct change in the distribution of land in Bahrain, nor in administrative transparency. This illustrates one of the traps that campaigners and activists often fall into. In campaigning terms, we tend to look for a direct 'cause and effect' reaction, and we ask what the impact of such an intervention may have been. But we may be missing an important point: some interventions are essential catalysts, but when an issue needs a long-term approach to change, with incremental steps along the way,

our campaigns may best be understood and appreciated for their ability to get the fire started or for the role they play in affecting direction.

The satellite images did exert a strong influence. They contributed – along with a wide range of other factors and forms of evidence – further documentation about abuses of power[9] to growing unrest in Bahrain about economic conditions and the lack of affordable housing, issues that became major grievances during the 2011 uprisings. By 2013, the problems relating to access to land and housing had increased, with "... an estimated 54,000 requests for government housing still pending for action".[10] According to a regional news source, nearly half of the people requesting such help had been on the waiting list for twenty years or more. Therefore, seven years after the original satellite photographs were circulated, the images were still being discussed. In 2013, a media outlet, Business Insider, published an article[11] reviewing the situation, pointing to the increased problems and producing new Google Earth satellite images showing that the problem had not only continued, it had got worse.

ABOVE:
Google Earth images from report circulated by activists, 2006.

8   William Wallis, Financial Times, November 24, 2006

9   A Gallup poll placed the housing shortage and economic problems at the centre of the uprising in Bahrain in 2011, where "41% of adults surveyed in Bahrain said there were times in the past 12 months when they did not have enough money to provide adequate housing".
     http://www.gallup.com/poll/146912/housing-shortage-stands-among-bahrain-woes.aspx

10   http://arabiangazette.com/bahrain-housing-shortage-crisis-deepens-20130305/

11   http://www.businessinsider.com/bahrain-satellite-photos-of-inequality-2013-4

Different approaches to visualising information will produce different degrees of involvement and engagement. The question is, how involved are the people you are trying to reach? Are they at the outer edges of your issue, needing to be drawn in? Or are they deeply involved in the issue and requiring a new perspective or new ways to engage?

The next three chapters will introduce a wide range of techniques for packaging arguments. Over 30 examples of inspiring ways in which you can visualise information have been collected. From those that rely more heavily on the visual: *Get the Idea*, to those that summarise arguments through the combination of data and visuals: *Get the Picture*, and finally those that place a greater emphasis on the data: *Get the Detail*. Each of these approaches gives an audience different levels of exposure and therefore demands a different level of engagement, from being intrigued to following a narrative, to taking a journey through data.

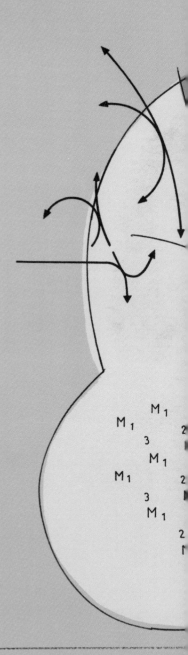

Get the Idea

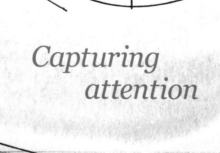

Capturing attention

Get the Idea:
capturing attention

What do we see when we look at these images, and what sort of effect do they have on us?

We suspect that they create a range of reactions as viewers start to connect the text with the image to create meaning and realise that the campaign is about female genital mutilation (FGM). Perhaps we think the image is completely inappropriate, an unsubtle metaphor trampling over a taboo to get our attention. Or perhaps we are uncomfortable with the contrast between a rose, a clichéd symbol for natural beauty, and what the metaphor, along with the crude stitching, represents.

The rose is a metaphor for the outcome of an act. This is a way of showing what cannot really be said in words, certainly not on a poster. There are three posters in the series – if we look at all three of them and we know about FGM, we can see that the images are more than a vague metaphorical representation: they refer to the three kinds of FGM that are practised.

At Tactical Tech, we have used Amnesty's rose image in a number of workshops on visual representation, and it's always interesting to see what a wide range of responses we get to it, from those that think it is incredibly powerful and choose it out of a number of examples as the most effective, to those that think it is an over-simplification and a cliché.

RIGHT:
Roses. Amnesty International Sweden.
Created by Volontaire. 2007.

Every year, two million girls suffer the pain of genital mutilation – a clear violation of their human rights. No government should continue to ignore this crime. Help us to stop violence against women. Give your support at www.amnesty.se

Help us to stop Female Genital Mutilation, stop violence against women. Support our work for human rights at www.amnesty.se

Whatever we think of the posters of roses, the approach illustrates some of the main features of the sort of visual advocacy that helps an audience *Get the Idea*:

▶ When it works, this approach can capture attention, because it challenges the values of the audience, breaks taboos and invites quick and immediate emotional reactions. While this sort of advocacy is provocative and controversial, it is not necessarily forceful; it can leave some space for interpretation and reflection by the viewer.

▶ This approach is difficult to get right. If badly conceived or executed, it can alienate or insult an audience. But when it works, the effect of such a campaign can be significant: it can spread quickly across media, be talked about and rapidly bring attention to an issue.

▶ These kinds of images pass on tiny packets of information about the issue, referring only obliquely to what people commonly think of as evidence, rather than presenting it directly. As provocations, such images mostly work as routes leading into a wider campaign where further information about the issue can be found. They are often designed to appeal to people who have not yet been exposed to the issue or who don't have a clear position.

The key characteristic of products that help audiences *Get the Idea* is the dominance of visual techniques. Such an image may give some information in the form of text, but principally they use a visual form to lead audiences to information about an issue, or into a larger campaign. Such visual tactics borrow from cultural, political and commercial communications practices. These forms of expression are often emotive, using shock, humour, subversion and metaphor, and have the effect of challenging the viewer, attempting to create a pivot for their opinions and ultimately their actions.

{ *Techniques:*

A. The Use of Visual Techniques to Help Audiences *Get the Idea*

Get the Idea is all about exposing people to an issue or inviting them to look further. Campaigners use many techniques to do this, combining information and design to make different appeals. We present a range of techniques commonly used by activists to help people *Get the Idea*.

▶ JUXTAPOSE

This campaign about adoption in India produced by Children of the World (India) Trust, uses analogy to make a point to the viewer.

The projected shadow of the profile of a woman holding a sleeping baby is juxtaposed with the shadow of a heavily pregnant woman, visually equating the two. This image teases at the difficult question of what childbearing and childrearing are, trying to bring to the surface the audience's opinions about whether caring for an adopted child is different from or less valid than the care a parent gives to her or his biological child.

The campaign attempts to challenge perceptions of adoption among people in India. It works on several levels, implying that all children – whether adopted or biological – need to be loved and cared for in the same way. It implies that all parents, whether adoptive or biological, can have the same feelings for their children. Whatever the reaction of the viewers and their own opinions, the campaign uses one simple powerful image, with a twist (just like Amnesty's rose) to convey a complex proposition and to ask the viewer a series of questions.

Just as written analogy or metaphor does, using a visual comparison or equivalence allows us to show similarities and resonances, in order to clarify or shed new light on what we're trying to say. This can help people understand a problem that is difficult to grasp, or act as a device giving depth to a story.

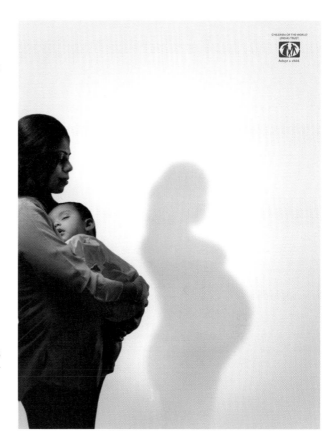

ABOVE:

Adopt a Child. Children of the World (India) Trust, with EuroRSCG India. 2008.

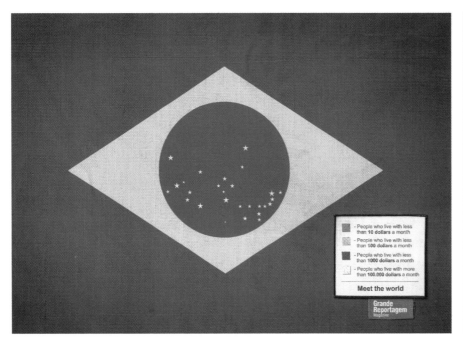

ABOVE:
Meet the World – Brazil, Somalia, China. Grande Raportagem.
Created by Icaro Doria/FCB Publicidade. 2005.

▶ SUBVERT

Many objects, symbols and places have certain social conventions associated with them, or have become iconic, with authority vested in them. *Meet the World* uses national flags in an unexpected way to subvert such meanings.

This series of flags was used in a promotional campaign for a now-discontinued Portuguese news magazine called Grande Raportagem.

Working for an advertising agency at the time, Icaro Doria, *Meet the World's* creator, came up with the idea almost accidentally: "I was flipping through the magazine [Grande Raportagem], trying to get a sense of it and I saw an article in it about female genital mutilation in Somalia. And there was a picture of the Somali flag right next to the data about how 90% of women there endure FGM and only 10% don't. And I couldn't avoid the fact that the data was very similar, in proportion to the graphic details of the flag: a small white

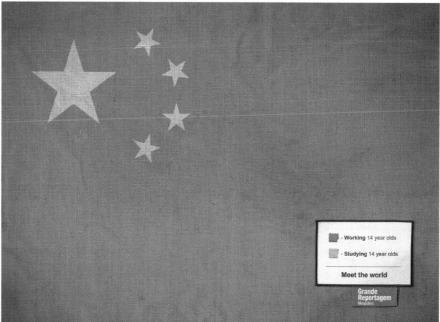

star in a big blue background. I found this very interesting. So I looked through the magazine to see if there were any other such issues from around the world that would be similarly interesting. I was looking for these kinds of patterns between data and their proportions to the images and blocks of colour on flags."

Doria produced a series of images of flags and showed them alongside facts that contradict what the flag represents. For example, the European Union flag has a key that shows the yellow stars as the number of oil producers and the majority blue background as the number of oil consumers. "The flags play with people's pride. You take a symbol of national pride and identity and show an aspect of that identity that people are not proud of. It really works", says Doria. Some countries prohibit tampering with their national flag[1], adding an additional layer of irreverent provocation to this campaign.

The flags were popular online and they also caught the attention of Brazilian officials: "When we launched this in the magazine, we had a picture of the Brazilian flag. Very soon after that, the Brazilian ambassador in Portugal wrote a letter to the magazine talking about how amazing Brazil is, how there is equality, how it is a great place for holidays, it has amazing beaches, and people are taken care of. Clearly it struck a nerve. It really hit home because he felt he had to write a letter saying all these other things about Brazil rather than facing the issues."

Subversion works because it shows viewers something they recognise and then, on closer inspection, flips their expectations of what the image is there for and what it is telling them.

---

1   More information on flag desecration: http://en.wikipedia.org/wiki/Flag_desecration

▶ INVERT

The *Children's World Map* is a billboard campaign by Save
the Children Sweden using a kind of inversion. Its depiction
of an atlas-style map with omissions is at once familiar and
strange. The map shows the countries that have protected
children's rights by making the corporal punishment of
a child a crime. Rather than highlighting or listing the
countries without such laws, their complete removal from
the traditional map creates a disorienting, drowned image
of the world, one that is alien to the viewer. The message is
clear: on our planet there are not many places where a child
is specifically protected from parental violence. The visual
expression of this idea centres on an unexpected absence
rather than a familiar presence. This is a much more
effective technique than the obvious one of highlighting the
world map in different colours to delineate which countries
do and do not have these laws: it uses its minimalism and
difference to tweak the curiosity of the viewer.

This 'less is more' technique can also be used as a
discipline. When we're trying to help audiences *Get the Idea*,
using a small slice of a much bigger story can draw them
in, make them curious. We should resist the temptation to
publish all the information at our disposal at the same time.
To paraphrase Bo Bergstrom, author of *Essentials of Visual
Communication* (2009), when a jazz musician in a busy
Parisian club wants to get everyone's attention, he
whispers quietly.

RIGHT:
Childrens' Map of the World.
Save the Children Sweden and Linus Östholm & Fredrik Lund/DDB
Stockholm 2009.

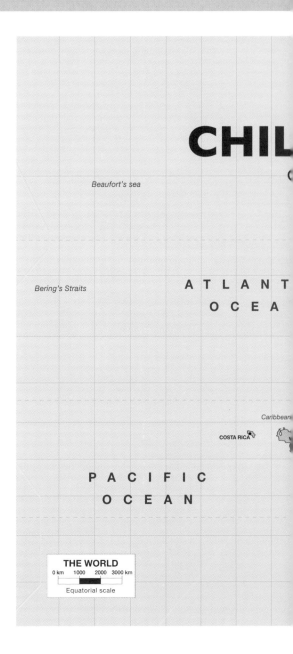

ARCTIC OCEAN

REN'S WORLD MAP

ries with a ban on corporal punishment of children

Beaufort's sea

Barent's sea

The north sea

ICELAND

SWEDEN
NORWAY   FINLAND

LATVIA

DENMARK

THE NETHERLANDS   POLAND
GERMANY
LUXEMBOURG   UKRAINE
AUSTRIA HUNGARY MOLDOVA
LIECHTENSTEIN   ROMANIA
CROATIA   BULGARIA
PORTUGAL SPAIN   ALBANIA
GREECE   CYPRUS
TUNISIA
ISRAEL

Bering's Straits

**PACIFIC
OCEAN**

TOGO
SOUTH SUDAN
REPUBLIC OF CONGO   KENYA

**INDIAN
OCEAN**

**ATLANTIC
OCEAN**

NEW ZEALAND

Save the Children
Sweden

▶ MATERIALISE

James Bridle is a British artist, who documents strikes by unarmed aerial vehicles (UAVs, commonly known as drones) on Afghanistan, Pakistan, Somalia, Yemen and countries the United States believes to be harbouring 'terrorists'.

These two very simple images look like satellite images, the kind we'd see on Google Earth or Google Maps. Bridle's Tumblr website[2] is full of images like these. Each of these images is a Google Maps satellite view of the location of a drone strike. The accompanying text reveals the date of the strike, its location, and the details of how many people were killed and who they were (if that information is available). The selection of images is based on information from the Bureau of Investigative Journalism which serves to materialise an otherwise abstract, hard-to-imagine problem and its impact. By using seemingly simple, even pedestrian images with sparsely written text, Bridle makes his point as succinctly as possible – each drone strike occurs in a real place, not somewhere alien, and there is documentation about the individuals killed in those attacks.

The images make visible what was invisible by taking facts that have already been documented by other people and turning them into simple images that serve to bring home those facts. Bridle also created an inexpensive, but

ABOVE (LEFT & RIGHT):
Images from *Dronestagram* blog. James Bridle. 2012.

RIGHT:
Drone Shadow 002. James Bridle. 2012.

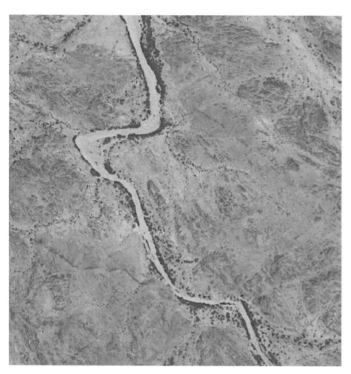

subtle and arresting effect when on the streets of London and Istanbul he drew scale diagrams of an MQ1 Predator Unmanned Aerial Vehicle [3], a common model in operation. In the presence of these outlines, audiences could see the actual dimensions of these drones for themselves, and consider what it means literally to live in their shadow.[4]

Bridle's simple gestures and all his work on exposing the costs of drone warfare, demonstrate how the misuse of high-end technologies in drones, are made invisible and remote.

If we don't know about them, we remain disengaged. He says of this work *In the Shadow of the Drone*:

"Those who cannot perceive the network cannot act effectively within it, and are powerless. The job, then, is to make such things visible. We all live under the shadow of the drone, although most of us are lucky enough not to live under its direct fire. But the attitude they represent – of technology used for obscuration and violence; of the obfuscation of morality and culpability; of the illusion of omniscience and omnipotence; of the lesser value of other people's lives; of, frankly, endless war – should concern us all."

2 James Bridles's tumblr: http://dronestagram.tumblr.com/

3 The General Atomics MQ-1 Predator is a type of unmanned aircraft used by the US Air Force. For more information see: http://en.wikipedia.org/wiki/General_Atomics_MQ-1_Predator

4 See Bridle's blog for further explanation of his work: http://booktwo.org/notebook/drone-shdadows/

▶ COMPARE

The infographic *Middle East: Who Backs Immediate
Ceasefire?* presents data about the states that supported or
opposed a ceasefire in the war between Israel and Lebanon
in 2006. It was created by The Independent newspaper,
and was published on its front page. The graphic shows
on the left the flags of those countries that voted for a
ceasefire and the right those that voted against.

   The designer has deployed two effective and
complementary design techniques. The first is the use of
flags to represent the countries. The flags are equal in size
and shape, unlike, for example, the images of countries
provided by maps, where the differences in size create a
visual inequity. The effect is to evoke ideas of sovereign
equality and democracy within the United Nations' system.
The second technique is the use of space to compare
the positions of each country. The visual effect invites
the viewer to question the flags' positions. The dramatic
contrast between left and right, for and against a ceasefire
– with some pieces taken out of the left side, resembling the
last pieces of a nearly complete jigsaw puzzle – highlights
the alignment of interests. Overall, it shows how a tiny
minority stands out from the great majority and hints at
the power imbalance that really exists.

   By translating political positions into spatial positions
and comparing them, the audience is invited to consider the
facts and to ask their own questions. It's hard to imagine a
newspaper headline or article that could work as effectively.

RIGHT:
Middle East: Who Backs an Immediate Ceasefire? The Independent. 2006.

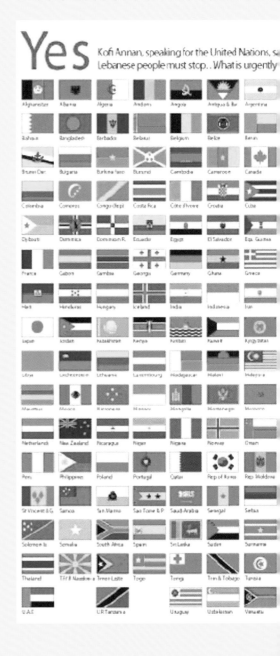

...diate cease-fire?

...rday: "The collective punishment of the ...is the immediate cessation of hostilities"

Australia　Austria　Azerbaijan　Bahamas

Bolivia　Bosnia & Herz.　Botswana　Brazil

Cent. Af. Rep.　Chad　Chile　China

Czech Rep.　D.P.R Korea　D.R Congo　Denmark

Estonia　Ethiopia　Fiji　Finland

Guatemala　Guinea　Guinea-Bissau　Guyana

Ireland　Italy　Jamaica

Latvia　Lebanon　Lesotho　Liberia

Mali　Malta　Marshall Is.　Mauritania

Bosnia (Myanmar)　Namibia　Nauru　Nepal

Palau　Panama　Papua N. G.　Paraguay

Russia　Rwanda　St Kitts & Nevis　Saint Lucia

Sierra Leone　Singapore　Slovakia　Slovenia

Sweden　Switzerland　Syria　Tajikistan

Turkmenistan　Tuvalu　Uganda　Ukraine

Vietnam　Yemen　Zambia　Zimbabwe

No

Margaret Beckett, Foreign Secretary, addressing the Cabinet yesterday, said:
"What people are really saying is they want a ceasefire with rockets still going into Israel"

Israel

UK

USA

▶ CONTRAST

This seemingly abstract image presents data from the US military 'SigActs' (Significant Actions) database that were obtained and made public by WikiLeaks. It shows civilians and military personnel killed in military engagements involving coalition forces in the Iraq war between 2004 and the end of 2009. Kamel Makhloufi is a French Canadian designer who created this work in his spare time. The images were republished in a number of high profile media outlets, including The New Yorker. "I never thought that it would have such an impact. It got so many comments after I posted it online. I'm still trying to find out why it was so popular!".

Makhloufi's images create two different narratives of the Iraq war, using the same original WikiLeaks data. The image on the right side shows the deaths as they were reported in the military's database: chronologically and plotted in rows, starting at the top left and running left to right. The result is a confusing mess of colours. The clearer image on the left presents the same data not chronologically but according to the nationality and characteristics of the people killed. This image reveals precisely what the other one conceals: the simple and memorable truth that civilian deaths massively outweigh military ones. Neither image would work as well on its own, but the differences between them allow people to contrast two narratives about the Iraq war.

This work also shows that it's possible to give meaning to huge amounts of data without having to select from or reduce it. By zooming out and abstracting it we can see new patterns that are meaningful to our understanding of the problem. The contrast between the two images makes the viewer think about the percentage of civilian deaths while asking questions about the problems of data presentation.

ABOVE:
Function. Kamel Makhloufi. 2010.

LEGEND:
Dark Blue   'Friendly troops'
Turquoise   Host nation troops
Orange   Iraqi Civilians /
Dark Grey   'Enemies'

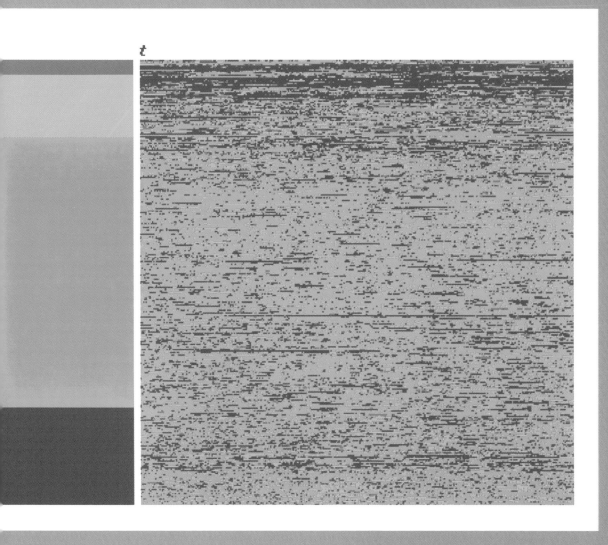

▶ ILLUMINATE

Across the Wall, Visualizing Palestine's map of bus routes uses seemingly mundane public data and represents it in an unusual way. Visualizing Palestine makes a series of substantial comments on the larger issue of Israeli settlements and the lack of freedom of movement for Palestinians.

Through this image, *Across the Wall* draws attention to the Green Line[5] – the internationally recognised border between Israel and the West Bank – and incursions into Palestinian territory by the Israeli West Bank barrier.[6]

The West Bank is Palestinian territory and Israeli settlements in it are considered illegal by the international community.[7] The map shows the direct bus routes among the settlements and Israeli territory. *Across the Wall* shows how Palestinians are either not allowed to use these buses or have to acquire special permits to use them while Israelis move freely in Israeli and occupied territory.

Ahmed Barclay of Visualizing Palestine says: "The maps are trying to communicate the continuity between Greater Jerusalem and Greater Israel... the West Bank settlements are seen as illegal but the route map shows how connected they are to Israel. We are trying to challenge the idea that the settlements are not part of Israel proper."

Barclay goes on to say "We did this – and actually all our work at Visualizing Palestine is the same – to talk to people who have a slight interest in the issue but who don't have the time to go into a lot of the reports and history and details. There is a limit to the media narrative, that doesn't give a full picture of what the situation is between Israel and Palestine, and so to present a more nuanced picture and to draw people into the issues, we created this map."

RIGHT:
Across the Wall. Visualizing Palestine. 2012. www.visualizingpalestine.org

5   The Green Line refers to the boundary lines drawn in green ink on a map in 1949 separating Israel from its neighbours.
     See: https://en.wikipedia.org/wiki/Green_Line_(Israel)

6   The Apartheid Wall is a barrier constructed by Israel separating Israel from the Palestinian West Bank.
     See: http://en.wikipedia.org/wiki/Israeli_West_Bank_barrier

7   Refer to: http://en.wikipedia.org/wiki/West_Bank

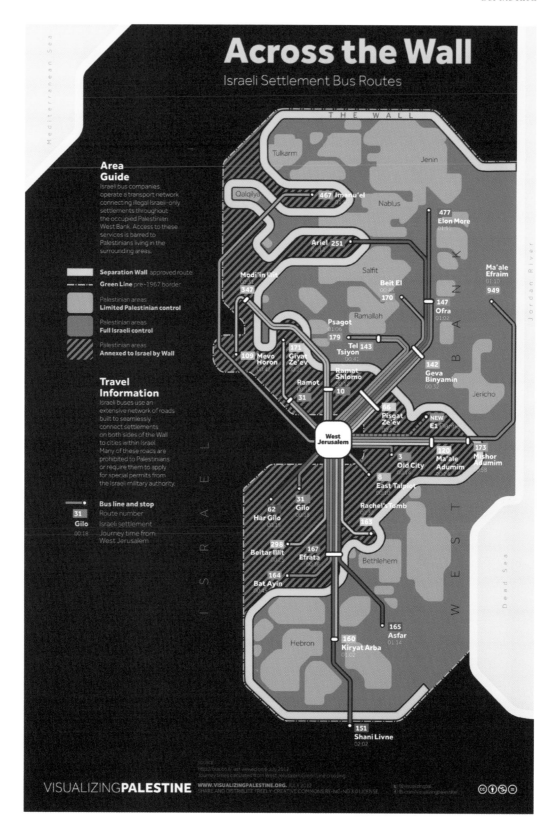

Across the Wall
Israeli Settlement Bus Routes

Area Guide

Israeli bus companies operate a transport network connecting illegal Israeli-only settlements throughout the occupied Palestinian West Bank. Access to these services is barred to Palestinians living in the surrounding areas.

Separation Wall approved route

Green Line pre-1967 border

Palestinian areas **Limited Palestinian control**

Palestinian areas **Full Israeli control**

Palestinian areas **Annexed to Israel by Wall**

Travel Information

Israeli buses use an extensive network of roads built to seamlessly connect settlements on both sides of the Wall to cities within Israel. Many of these roads are prohibited to Palestinians or require them to apply for special permits from the Israeli military authority.

Bus line and stop

31 Route number

Gilo Israeli settlement

00:18 Journey time from West Jerusalem

▶ PROVOKE

We are constantly selecting and excluding images and messages in our daily life; our visual environment is over-saturated. Humour and irony seem to be our Achilles' heel. It's hard to get it right but when we contextualise and hone humour for our audience it can be a very effective technique.

Is this yours? by Greenpeace was part of their public information work on plastic pollution in the Pacific Ocean. It is a snapshot of what looks to be a strangely vindictive diving expedition by environmentalists to find that toothbrush you just chucked away and never expected to see again. It is a simple joke, with a simple aim: to make us think about our plastic consumption and disposal, and to attract us to their campaign. It works because it is playful and uses wit to draw the viewer in, leaving us to imagine the rest of the story.

ABOVE:
Is this yours? Greenpeace. Photograph by Alex Hofford. 2007

PARODY

Some campaigns use humour that play on stereotypes and parody familiar conventions and symbols. In *Barbie, It's Over*, Greenpeace created an amusing story of Ken and Barbie's break-up as a way to draw people into the issue and a broader campaign. The famous male doll produced by the Mattel company, Ken, is the central character. The video – which you can watch at the link in the image caption – is a pastiche, combining a parody of television celebrity news with the stereotypical clichés of Barbie and Ken dolls. The breaking news-style video plays with these conventions, creating an amusing narrative in which Ken is traumatised to discover that Barbie has been destroying the rainforest for her packaging. The campaign itself is aimed at a range of toy makers, including Disney and Hasbro, but uses Ken and Barbie for its central story, thereby specifically targeting Mattel.

How to help people Get the Idea

Here are some questions to ask when developing a concept for a *Get the Idea* visual for a campaign.

▶ What are the reasons people are not talking about or acting on an issue?

▶ What contexts, symbols or situations can be used to represent our issue visually?

▶ What is the first, key, singular reaction we want our audience to have? What is the second immediate reaction?

▶ Where will the visual be presented – in real or virtual space – and who, apart from the target audience, will see the visual?

▶ How can we change the context of the problem and attract new audiences?

▶ How can our visual open up debate, controversy or curiosity rather than reinforcing a single answer or perspective?

ABOVE:
Ken finds some hard truths about Barbie. Greenpeace. http://vimeo.com/25832441

▶ INTRIGUE

Grabbing people's attention with arresting images is a technique often used in campaigning, though it is even more difficult to use effectively than humour. Jarring, arresting and shocking images are often used to try and attract interest and support. Many shocking images that have worked well to attract attention to an issue are re-enactments, showing only certain aspects of an event. Others provide context, or create an, 'a-ha' moment of revelation to reduce the discomfort of the viewer while still getting the idea across.

For example, the image of the albatross chick with his stomach full of plastic debris, that we explored in the case studies, pitches itself just on this line of 'bearable witnessing'. It works by taking the viewer on a visual journey that slowly leads them in to the shocking aspect of the image.

These are techniques that are used increasingly by commercial advertisers as a way of getting attention. Companies such as Benetton have made it a feature of their advertising campaigns. These techniques work for them, first because they are playing with social taboos as a way to create a shock reaction, but also because they are operating in a communications market where shock can get them free media attention. It may even make them more appealing to certain audiences, who are drawn to the supposed 'coolness' of breaking with convention. Despite the differences in aims we can learn a lot from the advertising industry's effective use of drama, visual playfulness and shock to influence their target audience.

Amnesty International's many successful visual campaigns are good examples of how this can work well. For example, Amnesty's *Making the Invisible Visible* campaign uses a visual trick to gain the attention of passers-by.

The technique used here is derived from lenticular or 3D printing. The image looks different according to the angle from which it is viewed. Pedestrians walking past see patterns on the railings, which then resolve, as they walk further, into a clear image of a face. The moment of intrigue comes both from the visual and when it becomes clear that the faces are those of people who have been imprisoned or murdered due to limits on freedom of expression. When passers-by read the stories their assumptions are challenged.

ABOVE:

Making the Invisible Visible. This image is of Troy Davis who was convicted of murdering a Georgia police officer in 1991 despite serious doubts about his guilt. Troy was executed in 2011. Creative Directors: Kirsten Rutherford, Lisa Jelliffe, Mentalgassi. Photo by Barry Mostert. Art for Amnesty. 2010.

What can go wrong?
The hazards of overdoing it

▶ VISUAL CLICHÉS

People who have followed climate change debates since the 1992 United Nations' Earth Summit in Rio de Janeiro[8] have probably seen a lot of pictures of sad-looking polar bears adrift on ice floes in the ocean.

The 1992 summit was an important global gathering for the environmental movement because it brought together governments, scientists, policy-makers and activists to make global commitments, based on scientific evidence, to protecting the environment. Since then there have been countless campaigns urging us to become aware of our harmful practices.

One of the most common images used in these is the polar bear. There is something quite attractive about a pristine, sparkling, icy landscape and a big furry animal. This imagery, however, has been overused as shorthand for the issue of climate change by activists and therefore may have lost its power with an audience. Decades of seeing polar bears in a variety of poses and states have changed the way we are affected by their plight and how much we think about our role in their fate. They have now become a visual shorthand for the issue of climate change.

This may sound cynical, but what we're trying to do is highlight one of the hazards of misusing the visual when we're trying to help audiences *Get the Idea*. If we overuse and abuse images and symbols they become stereotypes or clichés, and can have the opposite effect on the audience from that intended.

▶ STARK REALITIES

There is a difference between helping people *Get the Idea* in a short, subtle interaction, and relying too much on grabbing attention quickly, without offering useful or insightful information.

Thomas Keenan has written about the use of emotional motifs in advocacy, using his analysis of television footage of the Balkan and Iraq wars.[9] He talks about the way that emotive visual campaigns act on viewers in the same way as seeing footage of war and destruction does, by awakening shame.

"The dark side of revelation is overexposure. Sometimes we call it voyeurism, sometimes compassion fatigue, sometimes the obscenity of images or 'disaster pornography'... Obviously, this 'crisis' has important implications for the struggle for human rights, especially in an age when its traditional allies – the camera and the witness – have acquired unprecedented levels of public access, bordering at times on saturation."

He refers to shame as a sort of 'social contract' whereby we accept, as viewers, that there are terrible things going on and that we have a responsibility to feel something and act. This is how visual techniques that jar the senses, shock, horrify or even make us laugh operate.

However, there is a very real risk of turning these gross violations into something superficial through visual campaigns that merely raise awareness without doing much more. In these instances audiences remain mute spectators rather than being engaged participants. Hard-hitting visual campaigns can work, but it's difficult for them to do justice to the complexities of an issue.

8   For more information on the Earth Summit see: http://en.wikipedia.org/wiki/Earth_Summit
9   Thomas Keenan (2004), Mobilising Shame, The South Atlantic Quarterly 103:2/3, Spring/Summer 2004

ABOVE:
Homeless polar bear. WWF Finland and Havas Worldwide
Helsinki Oy. 2007.

Summary: drawing people to our issue

We have highlighted different kinds of visual representation that can work when we're conveying minimal information and making one simple point. There is an art to balancing the need to be concise and eye-catching with the desire to help an audience go deeper. The examples in this chapter are intended to inspire. The techniques we highlight are not intended to represent a comprehensive framework or formal categories, instead the aim is to provide a range of ideas to draw on or use in different combinations.

Helping our audience *Get the Idea* means making simple, eye-catching products that are based on substantial arguments, though these may not be spelled out. They are provocations and invitations to dig deeper. We need to be creative to help people *Get the Idea*, and we also need to know our issue and audience well, be able to back our visual presentation up with convincing evidence.

We need to work with graphic designers to make our images. But, when it comes to the design of the story and the selection of the information to be presented, these are processes that the advocate or activist communicating the information must be involved in. They understand best what needs to be said to whom, and what they want the audience to get from the product.

▶ Visualisation can turn the undefined, difficult to describe, complex and invisible into something a viewer can recognise and relate to. This can create a quick bridge between the problem we are trying to describe and the individual or group of people who may be interested in it. It can allow us to lead people into a complex problem through a simple story or hook.

▶ Visual information is a flexible and efficient way of communicating. There are many possible approaches to visually representing any issue. A visualisation can cut straight to the point of a matter very effectively, or raise an issue without being too direct; for example, about something taboo, sensitive or even dangerous.

▶ Attention-grabbing techniques such as shock, humour and even beauty become stronger in a visual context, with different strengths from those they'd possess in a written text.

▶ Visual information opens up new ways of communicating that are not otherwise possible. It enables the creation of something distinctive that stands out and is memorable to audiences because it creates a new sort of experience for them. Visualisation can be a fresh form of expression, enabling new forms of debate and participation.

▶ Visual information creates alternative perspectives so that the audience can explore, identify with and participate in an issue. It can help people recognise their own point of view and affirm the relevance of an issue to them, or it can give them space to think and decide for themselves.

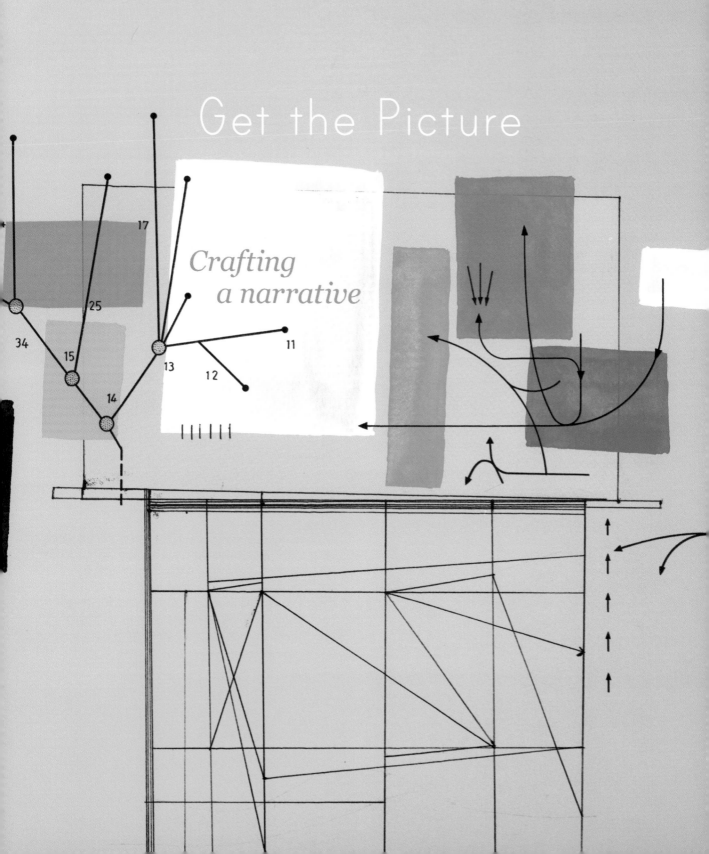

Get the Picture

Crafting a narrative

Get the Picture: crafting a narrative

Once we've got people's attention and helped them *Get the Idea*, what's next?

As activists who work with information, our tendency is to want to tell the whole story and show all the work we've done. In some cases, it may be fair or necessary to publish everything we know, but often this approach is not very effective. Regardless of the rigour and skill that go into data collection, and regardless of the quality of research, Non-Governmental Organisations (NGOs) are awash with 60-page reports that very few people have ever read; they tend to collect dust on the shelves of like-minded organisations. In five years of talking about this with NGOs from around the world, we've only ever been met with rooms full of people nodding in agreement when we talk about the need to go beyond the '60-page report'.

If we want people to understand and act on issues, the challenge is much greater than just the problem of representation and beautification. It's not enough to let the people who design our reports add more white space or a few full-page photographs. We need to find concise ways of telling stories that strengthen the information we're trying to get across by presenting it well and beautifully, but without dumbing down the issues. We need to give people helpful short-cuts that increase their understanding of our key points, orient them within a particular perspective and entice them to explore our issues further.

By telling stories effectively, with high-quality data, delivered in a clear and compelling way, we can increase people's understanding and focus their attention on the most pressing or revealing aspects of an issue.

We can:
▶ Present a brief visual executive summary.
▶ Help people to grasp a problem by understanding its context or scale, how it came about, how it compares to other issues, or how urgent it is.
▶ Illustrate a complex point, much as we do when reaching for pen and paper and sketching it out, something many people do instinctively.
▶ Help people to see different perspectives, and illuminate an issue in fresh ways.

At Tactical Tech workshops we have seen that when given a data set and the task of visualising it, most people will either draw a map, a bar graph or a pie chart. These are familiar visual organising principles that we can rely on without having to invent something new. There's nothing wrong with maps and bar charts. We see them so frequently because we often need them and they're easy to use. However, the hard question we have to ask ourselves before we use them is, "Is this the best organising principle for the information we have and the story we are trying to tell?" In order to start thinking differently about representing information, we need to consider what we really intend to achieve, rather than just falling back on our habits or basic abilities.

Often we use visuals as a way to help us put things into perspective by manipulating context and using comparison. We can make things more meaningful to people if we can help them move from an abstract awareness to something they can grasp and relate to. In this chapter, we suggest eight organising principles that can help us tell evidence-based stories that shift people's perceptions.

Techniques:

Get the Picture is all about crafting stories with high quality information to increase an audience's understanding of an issue and to focus their attention on its most revealing or pressing aspects.

▶ ASSOCIATIONS

The environmental organisation Toxics Link focuses on the ways in which toxic pollution affects people living in India. In order to promote understanding of the scale of the problem of pollution in a city such as Delhi, and to look at its impact on different types of communities, they decided to experiment with a graphic novel format.
As Ravi Agarwal, Executive Director of Toxics Link, says:
   "Graphic novels are contemporary and address a wide range of audiences. They can help make complex stories easier to relate to. A good visualisation can stay in the mind for a long time and make the case very effectively. They are closer to how most of us retain information". The graphic novel, *Our Toxic World – A guide to hazardous substances in our everyday lives* [1], combines a strong storyline about fictional characters with detailed information on pollution-related problems and their impact on individuals.
   The graphic novel was placed in bookstores. Agarwal said one of the things that really worked about this was that it "... occupied a new niche normally not provided to 'awareness materials'. It helped in reaching out to audiences which one would normally find hard to access".
   The graphic novel is 160 pages long, and took eight months to produce.

RIGHT:
Panel from Our Toxic World. Toxics Link.

1   'Our Toxic World – A guide to hazardous substances in our everyday lives', Aniruddha Sen Gupta, Toxics Link, Sage, New Delhi, India, 2010.

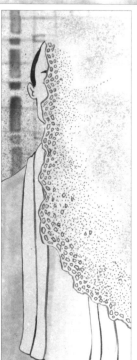

▶ CONNECTIONS

Walk This Way is an infographic produced by Good
Magazine, exploring the issue of water consumption, in
particular an individual's water footprint. In presenting
the information the designer has chosen two ways to
describe water consumption: the direct consumption
of water through visible, everyday acts such as flushing
a toilet, and the indirect, invisible consumption of water
through such processes as the production of beef. For each
water consumption unit, an alternative is presented that
automatically introduces the idea of choice. For example,
look at the difference in the number of units of water used
to produce a beef steak as opposed to a baked potato. The
choices are also mapped over a typical day, from getting up,
to breakfast, to lunch and so on. Framing the information
in this way invites the reader to consider her or his own day,
the options available and the choices made.

RIGHT:
Walk This Way. Fogelson Lubliner, GOOD. Good Magazine. 2009.

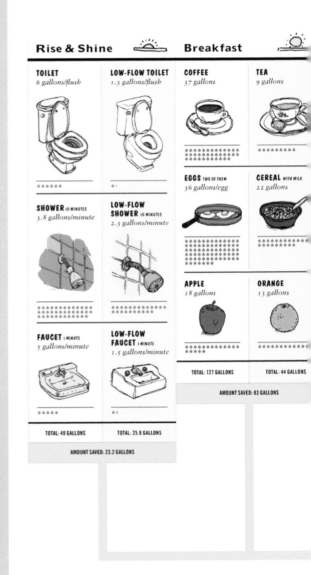

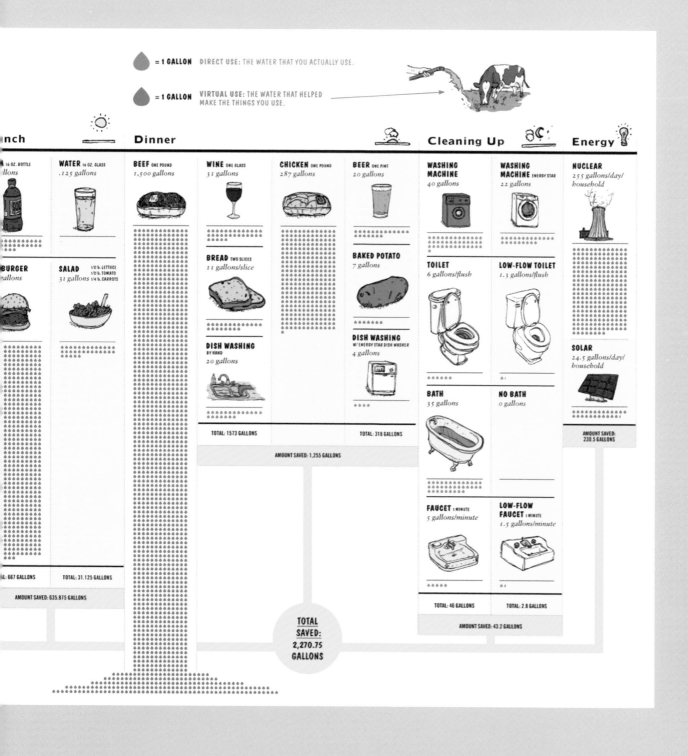

= 1 GALLON   **DIRECT USE:** THE WATER THAT YOU ACTUALLY USE.

= 1 GALLON   **VIRTUAL USE:** THE WATER THAT HELPED MAKE THE THINGS YOU USE.

nch   **Dinner**   **Cleaning Up**   **Energy**

16 OZ. BOTTLE
llons

WATER 16 OZ. GLASS
.125 gallons

BEEF ONE POUND
1,500 gallons

WINE ONE GLASS
31 gallons

CHICKEN ONE POUND
287 gallons

BEER ONE PINT
20 gallons

WASHING MACHINE
40 gallons

WASHING MACHINE ENERGY STAR
22 gallons

NUCLEAR
255 gallons/day/household

BURGER
allons

SALAD 1/2 lb. LETTUCE
31 gallons 1/2 lb. TOMATO
1/4 lb. CARROTS

BREAD TWO SLICES
11 gallons/slice

BAKED POTATO
7 gallons

TOILET
6 gallons/flush

LOW-FLOW TOILET
1.3 gallons/flush

DISH WASHING
BY HAND
20 gallons

DISH WASHING
W/ ENERGY STAR DISH WASHER
4 gallons

SOLAR
24.5 gallons/day/household

BATH
35 gallons

NO BATH
0 gallons

AMOUNT SAVED:
230.5 GALLONS

TOTAL: 1573 GALLONS

TOTAL: 318 GALLONS

AMOUNT SAVED: 1,255 GALLONS

FAUCET 1 MINUTE
5 gallons/minute

LOW-FLOW FAUCET 1 MINUTE
1.5 gallons/minute

L: 667 GALLONS

TOTAL: 31.125 GALLONS

AMOUNT SAVED: 635.875 GALLONS

TOTAL SAVED: 2,270.75 GALLONS

TOTAL: 46 GALLONS

TOTAL: 2.8 GALLONS

AMOUNT SAVED: 43.2 GALLONS

BILL OF HEALTH

The prognosis for health care in America isn't positive. Many people are uninsured and many more lack the level of care they need. Collectively, we cough up trillions to keep citizens well, but our health indicators lag behind other nations that spend far less. Here is a detailed diagnosis of the problem.

A LOOK AT WHAT'S WRONG:

THE UNITED STATES SPENDS $2 TRILLION ON HEALTH CARE ANNUALLY.

THAT MEANS MORE THAN $6,700 IS SPENT ANNUALLY ON EACH AMERICAN'S HEALTH CARE.

PERCENTAGE BREAKDOWN BY SOURCE OF FUNDS:

36%	35%	15%	11%	4%
Private health insurance	Federal government	Out-of-pocket payments	State & local government	Other private funds

COST BREAKDOWN BY TYPE OF EXPENDITURE:

- $621.7 billion Clinical services
- $611.6 billion Hospital
- $338.6 billion Other
- $258.8 billion Medical products and drugs
- $169.3 billion Nursing homes

SAMPLE: GOVERNMENT SPENDING

$313 billion = cost of Medicaid + Medicare in 2001

$559 billion = cost of Medicaid + Medicare in 2007

$1.26 trillion = projected cost in 2017

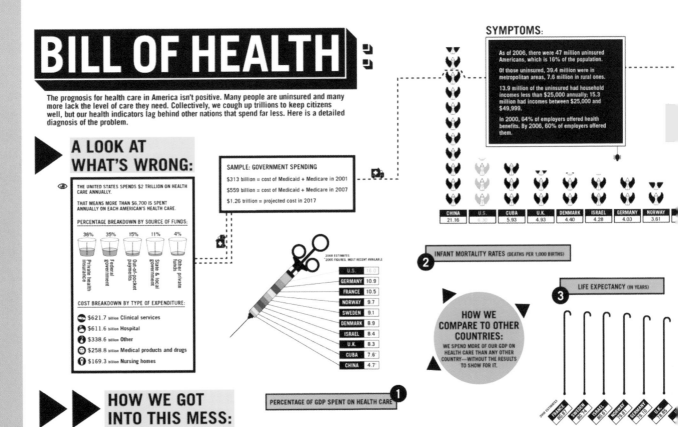

2008 ESTIMATES
*2005 FIGURES, MOST RECENT AVAILABLE

U.S.	16.0
GERMANY	10.9
FRANCE	10.5
NORWAY	9.7
SWEDEN	9.1
DENMARK	8.9
ISRAEL	8.4
U.K.	8.3
CUBA	7.6*
CHINA	4.7*

PERCENTAGE OF GDP SPENT ON HEALTH CARE — 1

SYMPTOMS:

As of 2006, there were 47 million uninsured Americans, which is 16% of the population.

Of those uninsured, 39.4 million were in metropolitan areas, 7.6 million in rural ones.

13.9 million of the uninsured had household incomes less than $25,000 annually; 15.3 million had incomes between $25,000 and $49,999.

In 2000, 64% of employers offered health benefits. By 2006, 60% of employers offered them.

CHINA	U.S.	CUBA	U.K.	DENMARK	ISRAEL	GERMANY	NORWAY
21.16	6.30	5.93	4.93	4.40	4.28	4.03	3.61

INFANT MORTALITY RATES (DEATHS PER 1,000 BIRTHS) — 2

LIFE EXPECTANCY (IN YEARS) — 3

HOW WE COMPARE TO OTHER COUNTRIES:

WE SPEND MORE OF OUR GDP ON HEALTH CARE THAN ANY OTHER COUNTRY—WITHOUT THE RESULTS TO SHOW FOR IT.

FRANCE 80.87	SWEDEN 80.74	ISRAEL 80.61	NORWAY 79.81	GERMANY 79.10	U.S.

2008 ESTIMATES

HOW WE GOT INTO THIS MESS:

1800s: Lumber, mining, and railroad companies offer health care to workers to keep up production.

1901: The beginning of organized medicine. The American Medical Association becomes the national organization of state and local associations.

1910s: Progressive reformers argue for health insurance and the American Association for Labor Legislation organizes the first national conference on "social insurance."

1930s: The 1935 National Labor Relations Act, requiring management to bargain with labor over "wages and conditions," is enacted and soon becomes a catalyst for employer-based health benefits.

1935: The Social Security Act passes without any included health-insurance benefits.

1940s: During WW II, employers attract workers with health-insurance benefits in lieu of raises.

1945: President Truman's plan for a national health program is attacked by the AMA and called a Communist plot by a House of Representatives subcommittee.

1946: The Blue Cross Commission, the early national organization of Blue Cross Plans, is created.

After WW II: For-profit insurers enter market in competition with Blue Cross, attracting young and healthy workers with low rates.

1950s: Nonprofit Blue Cross and Blue Shield organizations create a giant insurance pool, keeping costs predictable and relatively low.

1955: Health insurance which provided coverage for less than 10% of the population in 1940, covers nearly 70% in 1955.

1959: Congress enacts the Federal Employees Health Benefits Act; a Federal Employees Health Program open enrollment is held in 1960. FEHP now covers more than 9 million employees, retirees, and their families.

1965: Medicare and Medicaid are signed into law.

late 1970s: Insurance coverage peaks as 85% of Americans have some form of private health care coverage.

1997: The State Children's Health Insurance Program is launched to provide health coverage to uninsured children.

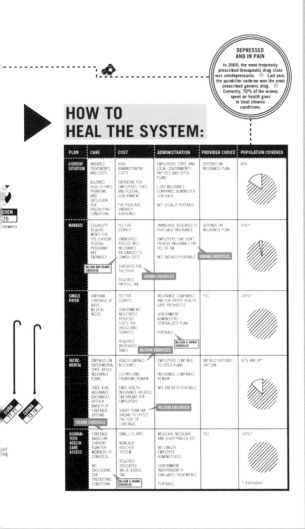

▶ REMEDIES

In the years leading up to the passage of healthcare reform in the US[2], there were several attempts to clarify the extent of the problems in the US health care system. *Bill of Health* is a visual attempt to explain the political and technical debate in the US about the financing of the health system. There are two mutually reinforcing narrative threads in the infographic, produced by Good Magazine: the first describes the problem and how it might be fixed. The second shows why the issue needs attention, showing that despite the huge amount of money spent, health care in the United States compares unfavourably to that in other countries, on infant mortality and life expectancy, for example. This infographic uses strong visual cues to create many entry points for the viewer helping them through a large amount of data and easing the feeling of being overwhelmed, while sustaining interest in the graphic. This infographic also gives context to the evolution of the problem, laying out a timeline of major events and influences on US health care legislation. This infographic does not appeal to everyone as it is quite complex, but is a good example of how to try and get a multi-layered story to flow if you need to try and fit a lot of information into one graphic.

LEFT:
Bill of Health. Karlssonwilker inc, NYC. GOOD, published by Good Magazine, 2008.

2   Two federal statues were enacted in 2010 aimed at reforming the US health care system. For an overview see:
http://en.wikipedia.org/wiki/Health_care_reform_in_the_United_States

▶ CORRELATIONS

Italian information designers Francesco Franchi and Laura Cattaneo are well-known for their very distinctive style. Their infographics tell complex stories through visual representation. This is not something that every reader likes. The educational style makes the reader work to learn how to read what is front of them. This sort of approach, however, is widely used in the print media in effort to present issues from different perspectives and break up standard reporting.

Francesco Franchi talks about the graphic designer inside the newsroom as "an important player who can act like an interpreter". He talks about what he calls visual journalism as a "combination between graphics and narratives. So it is at the same time representation, but also an interpretation of reality to develop an idea."[3]

If done well, this can be an engaging format for readers who are more comfortable grasping things visually. This example, on disarmament, explores the details of the growing arms trade. In the centre it shows the top ten importing and exporting states. The panel on the right shows a series of facts about the types of arms sold by each of the top ten companies (top right). It compares the biggest producers of arms and how much of the market each dominates (middle right). It also compares the biggest consumers to each other.

RIGHT:
Altro che disarmo, IL 20. Sara Deganello and Francesco Franchi. Illustrations by Laura Cattaneo. IL/Il Sole 24 Ore. 2010.

3   Francesco Franchi, On Visual Storytelling and New Languages in Journalism, www.gestalten.tv/motion/francesco-franchi

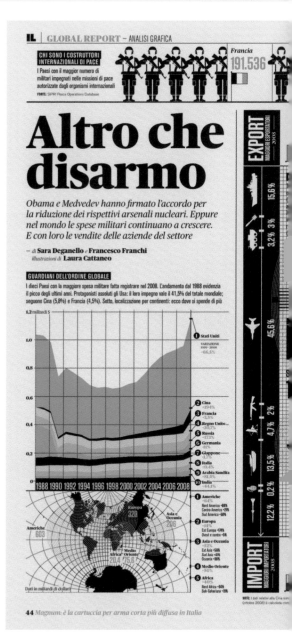

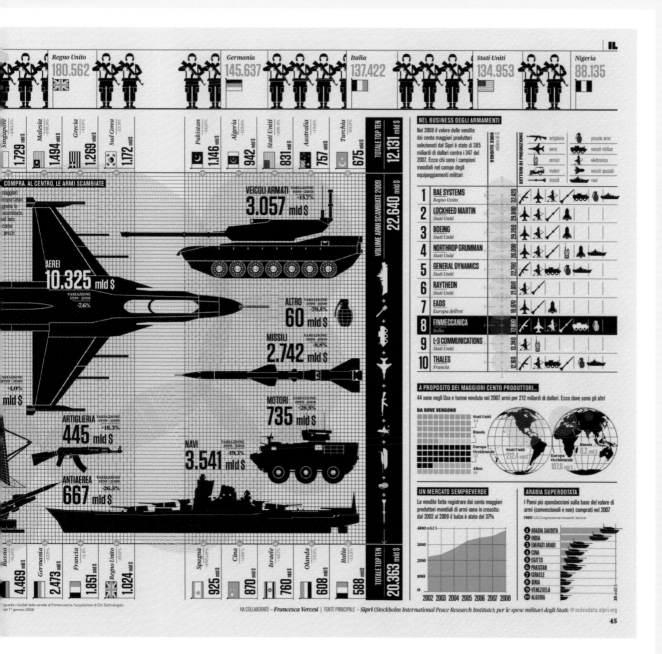

DOCUMENTS THAT I NEEDED TO TRAVEL OUTSIDE PALESTINE *Majdi Hadid*   112

DOCUMENTS THAT I NEE

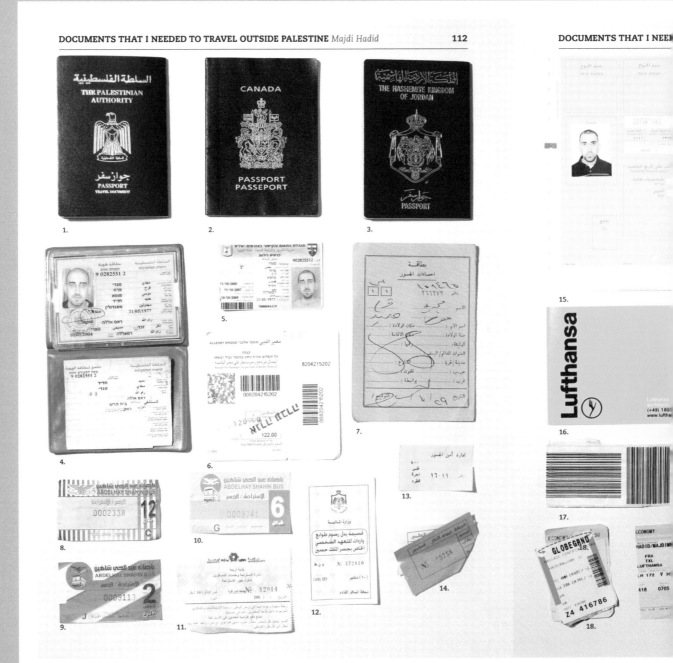

RAVEL OUTSIDE PALESTINE *Majdi Hadid*   **113**

1. **Palestinian Passport**
   valid for three years
2. **Canadian Passport**
   valid for five years
3. **Jordanian Passport**
   Expired since 1996, almost all Palestinians have one like this, the number starts with 'T' for temporary
4. **Palestinian Identification Card**
   You cannot leave your house without it. The green colour for Palestinian and the blue ID for the Israelis
5. **'Magnetic Card'**
   another ID but this one is issued by the Israeli authorities. It facilitates transportation around the country and will allow you to apply for special permission to travel through Israel
6. **Tax Paper to cross the Israeli border**
   'Allenby Bridge' 126 NIS – *New Israeli Shekels* (c. € 24,–). It's the only way out for all the people in the West Bank
7. **The green card**
   Only for the Jordanian side. They write the entry and departure dates in and out of Jordan
8. **Bus ticket for one person from Allenby Bridge to Jericho** 12 NIS (c. €2,–)
9. **Single luggage ticket from Jericho to the Allenby Bridge** 2 NIS (c. € 0,50)
10. **Bus ticket for one person from Jericho to the Allenby Bridge** 12 NIS (c. €2,–)
11. **Ticket to enter the rest area in Jericho**
    There you take a bus to *Al Alami checkpoint* and then you transfer to another bus in front of the Israeli soldiers
12. **Tax paper for the Jordanian border**
    10 JD – *Jordanian Dinar* (c. €11,–)
    When you pay it you sign the other side, not to stay in Jordan for more than 30 days, otherwise you have to contact the local government office
13. **Ticket for leaving Jordanian bridge**
    400 fils (c. € 0,50)
14. **Two tickets** 8 NIS (c. € 1,50)
    Obtained from no man's land in the middle of the two bridges, where you collect your luggage to go to the Jordanian side
15. **Special permission** 70 NIS (c. € 14,–)
    Sold in case you don't have a valid Palestinian Passport, or if your Passport has been issued for less than 30 days from your travelling date; that's how long it takes to register the passport from the Palestinian Authority to the Israeli side
16. **Round trip ticket Amman-Jordan to Frankfurt Germany** (c. € 500,–)
17. **Luggage tag** from Amman to Jordan
18. **Boarding Pass** from Amman to Frankfurt
19. **Boarding Pass** from Frankfurt to Amman

▶ PORTRAITS

Travel documents I needed to travel outside Palestine is a montage from a book called *Subjective Atlas of Palestine*. It plainly displays the nineteen documents that the creator of this work, Majdi Haddid, needed in order to travel outside Palestine. Haddid takes a well-known political problem and explains it at a highly personal level. The amount of documentation Haddid needs and the way it is displayed implies an act of interrogation – something he undoubtedly experienced and chooses to represent through the image.

As viewers, we can identify with this by comparing it to the relative ease and simplicity of our own travel experiences. This is one of over 30 artworks in the book, which collects personal maps in order to create an alternative kind of atlas of a long-standing issue.

Annelys de Vet, the Dutch artist who coordinated the project says, "a story is never complete and always more layered than at first glance, especially when dealing with the notion of identity. With the kind of mapping that is done in these subjective atlases you can experience the bigger story, without explanation". [4]

LEFT:
Travel documents I needed to travel outside Palestine. Majdi Hadid.
In Subjective Atlas of Palestine. Annelys de Vet (ed.) 2007.

4   Subjective Atlas of Palestine, edited and designed by Annelys de Vet, www.annelysdevet.nl/palestine.

▶ PERCEPTIONS

In trying to understand an issue, we are often asked to comprehend measurements that are difficult to grasp. This could be because the scale means nothing to us, or it could be because we are being asked to try and understand something we have no direct experience of or way to map.

The BBC developed *How Big Really*[5] to help people understand the impact of large-scale environmental problems, such as the size of the Great Pacific Garbage Patch or the BP oil spill.

They did this by using a geo-spatial reference that has relevance for the user. In this example, we can see the size of the area destroyed by the Pakistan floods of 2010 mapped on to a specific postcode in the UK.

Earlier versions of this have existed as mash-ups on the internet, like the chilling mapplet that allows the viewer to see the area affected by devastating explosions, from "Little Boy", the bomb dropped by the USA on Hiroshima in 1945, to an asteroid's collision with the earth.[6]

RIGHT:
How Big Really? BBC. 2010.

5   Explore the BBC's How Big Really website: www.howbigreally.com
6   Test out the mapplet application called Ground Zero created by Carlos Labs at: http://www.carloslabs.com/projects/200712B/GroundZero.html

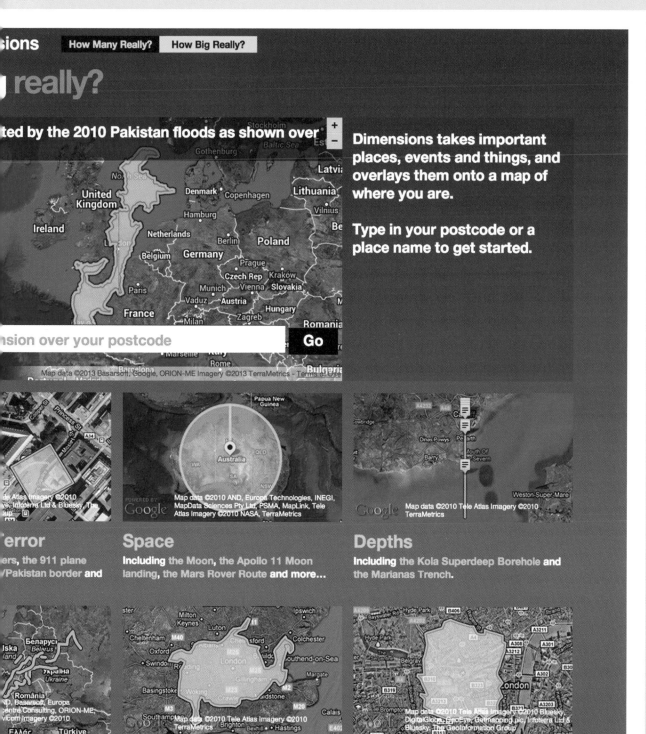

…sions   How Many Really?   How Big Really?

…g really?

…ted by the 2010 Pakistan floods as shown over

Dimensions takes important places, events and things, and overlays them onto a map of where you are.

Type in your postcode or a place name to get started.

…nsion over your postcode   **Go**

Map data ©2013 Basarsoft, Google, ORION-ME Imagery ©2013 TerraMetrics - Terms of Use

…e Atlas Imagery ©2010
…ve, Infoterra Ltd & Bluesky. The
…up

Map data ©2010 AND, Europa Technologies, INEGI, MapData Sciences Pty Ltd, PSMA, MapLink, Tele Atlas Imagery ©2010 NASA, TerraMetrics

Map data ©2010 Tele Atlas Imagery ©2010 TerraMetrics

…error

…ers, the 911 plane …/Pakistan border **and**

Space

Including the Moon, the Apollo 11 Moon landing, the Mars Rover Route **and more…**

Depths

Including the Kola Superdeep Borehole **and** the Marianas Trench.

Map data ©2010 Tele Atlas Imagery ©2010 TerraMetrics

Map data ©2010 Tele Atlas Imagery ©2010 Bluesky, DigitalGlobe, GeoEye, Getmapping plc, Infoterra Ltd & Bluesky, The GeoInformation Group

…ds

…l of China, the first …Pyramids of Giza **and**

Environmental Disasters

Including the Gulf Oil Spill, the Great Pacific Garbage Patch, Exxon Valdez **and more…**

Festivals and Spectacles

Including the Glastonbury festival, St Peter's Basilica and Square, the Burning Man festival **and more…**

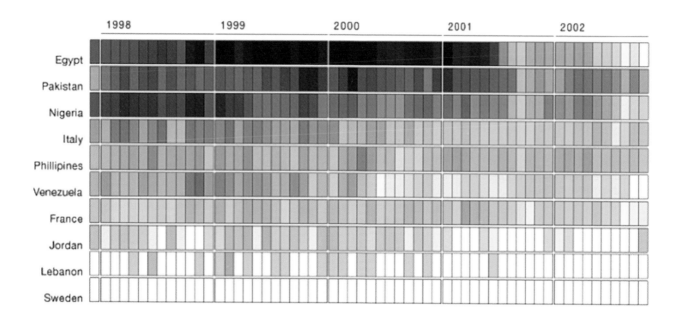

▶ INTERACTIONS

Dutch design studio Catalogtree visually represented information linking the parking fines incurred by diplomats in the city of New York with broader issues of corruption. An initial visualisation of this data was created in the form of a table that was published in The New York Times, see above. This is a strong and simple design that clearly shows patterns and enables the viewer to analyse of the findings at a glance. Its simplicity makes it easy to read, illustrating 141,369 data points within a single image.

Helping audiences to *Get the Picture* is about providing them with enough information to draw their own conclusions. The viewer can read the image above, and quickly get the gist, focusing for example on the darker shades in the top left – Egypt, Pakistan and Nigeria – or reflect on the different patterns of the three European countries – Italy, France and Sweden – and how this relates to what we know about these countries, or ask questions such as, "what happened in 2002?"

In other pieces based on the same data set, Catalogtree worked more experimentally, through a series of posters. *The Flocking Diplomats* series shows different aspects of the data in increasingly abstract but comprehensible formats. FD-4, for example, shown left, is an image treemap showing photographs of the 100 places where parking fines were most frequently issued to diplomats. Turning the list of violations into real places appeals to our sense of curiosity, as we start to wonder why some places make the top 100. By exploring the same data through a number of different visualisations we get a variety of views of the same picture.

LEFT:

Catalogtree images from the *Flocking Diplomat* series. 2008. The data is based on a paper by Ray Fisman and Edward Miguel, *Corruption, Norms, and Legal Enforcement: Evidence from Diplomatic Parking Tickets,* published in the Journal of Political Economy in December 2007.

ABOVE:

Diplomatic Parking Violations. Catalogtree. 2008

What can go wrong: the limits of visualisation

▶ PUTTING TOGETHER THE FACTS

With increased access to data visualisation tools and mapping software, it is now possible to trade up from the pie charts and bar graphs offered in our everyday spreadsheet programme to more descriptive visualisations. However, the question remains – what next? How does the presentation of data in a visualisation or on a map contribute to our campaign?

Simple mapping and data visualisation tools can serve as an introduction to seeing information in a whole new light, prompting us to start asking questions and developing our own idea of what it means to communicate visually with numbers. However, we are witnessing an explosion of information graphics today, as a result of the sheer quantity of text-based information that we are all exposed to. See Phil Gyford's infographic about infographics (right).

The development of easily accessible data visualisation software results in what Megan McCardle of The Atlantic calls the "plague of infographics". [7] Some infographics we come across online can be quite glitzy-looking and impressive at first glance; others will put us off instantly with their vast webs of connections, endless pie charts or tacky clip-art-like visualisations. Certain infographics may be based on questionable or misleading data that we don't spot because we're overwhelmed by the image. Others make us feel exasperated; why would anyone want to spend their time making an infographic to show the overlaps and distinctions between a) the number of people who like pies, and b) the number of people who hate circles?

Bluntly put, does every piece of data need to be visualised as an infographic, just because it can be? Easy to make and readily shareable, infographics have become the flotsam of the internet – they are everywhere, they can be annoying and they can be easily forgettable in the slew of information around us. If we are going to make them we need to be sure we understand why.

RIGHT:
Infographic. Phil Gyford. 2010.

7   'Ending the Infographic Plague', Megan Mcardle. The Atlantic, 23 December 2011.

▶ THE MYTH OF MAPS

The same problem exists for maps and their overuse, this has been highlighted specifically in the *Dead Ushahidi Project*, a map of defunct or 'dead' maps. Ushahidi (meaning 'witness' in Kiswahili) is a platform that uses crowd-mapping to create documentation of events. It was first developed to expose post-electoral violence in Kenya in 2007-2008, and has since become one of the most accessible digital documentation and reporting platforms allowing rapid data collection around a particular event, such as electoral violence or natural disasters.

This easy-to-use platform has enabled some important initiatives, but it has also created a large number of maps that on closer inspection don't really work. The problem with mapping and visualisation tools can be that by starting with the solution we may be tricked into overlooking the real problem. As the project says:

> "There is an increasing number of Ushahidi maps that are set up with little thought as to the why, what, who, and how... Using crowdsourcing technology such as Ushahidi maps without doing the strategic and programmatic ground work is unlikely to work, or to change much. Trying to crowdscource a map without a goal or strategy leaves us with just a map, which will soon be a dead map."[8]

The Dead Ushahidi Project is making a critical point – one that we have reiterated in this guide, too: that our choice of the kind of visuals or technology we want to use to display information must be driven by a thorough understanding of our reach, network, resources and skills. Whilst Ushahidi is a great platform, our choices must grow out of our broader strategies for advocacy: who we want to influence and how we want them to engage with our content.

ABOVE:
The Dead Ushahidi Crowdmap showing where 'dead' crowdmaps lie. A dead map is one that has not had any reports in 12 months, the numbers of reports in time-bound events is extremely small compared to the population affected, or where there are no reports submitted at all.

The Dead Ushahidi Project makes a critical point, challenging the use of mapping that doesn't have a clear strategic vision or direction for using information in advocacy.

■ ALL CATEGORIES

■ REPAIR REPORTS: BROKEN THINGS THAT GO UNFIXED.

■ CRIME, VIOLENCE, AND OTHER SAD THINGS

■ YEAH NATURE: WHERE HUMANS HAVE KILLED THE EARTH AND SUCH

■ AGGREGATING STUFF

■ HEART-WARMING CIRCLE JERKS: HELP YOUR NEIGHBOR, BUT NOT REALLY.

■ TIME-BOUND EVENTS (WITH ABYSMAL REPORTING VOLUME.)

■ HEALTH, DISEASES, STOCKOUTS AND SUCH. EXCEPT FOR WHEN THEY WEREN'T.

Summary:
telling stories with information

Get the Picture is about creating a visual summary of your argument, finding a way audiences can relate to and understand the message.[9] While maps and data visualisations are relatively easy to make, they often do not convey an engaging narrative; they are essentially tools and platforms rather than vehicles for story-telling. As we've shown in this chapter, there are many other possibilities for telling a captivating story. The challenge lies in thinking carefully about what we're trying to achieve, who we're trying to influence and how to develop a coherent storyline; what brings depth and integrity to these is knowing the strengths and limitations of the data. When presenting information to help people *Get the Picture* we need to ask hard questions about what exactly we want to display and why. This process can help us think strategically about the kind of influence we are trying to have.

▶ By comparison with conventional ways of presenting evidence, such as 60-page reports, a visual executive summary can help audiences understand and relate to our issue quickly.

▶ The danger in creating a visual summary is that the issue can be dumbed down; the data can be shoehorned in to fit the most convenient argument: make sure that imagery and nice design don't become substitutes for a strong argument, and that there is a story that appeals to the viewer.

▶ Aesthetics and design certainly matter, but the biggest challenge in creating an infographic is to get the narrative right. There is a range of familiar narrative types we can use to tell stories that inform, and other narratives that we can use to help our audiences build themselves into an issue and explore it.

▶ In designing an information product, we need to find the best organising principle for the information, rather than the most comfortable or convenient for us. We can find organising principles by thinking about what our audiences need to know in order to change their perception of an issue.

▶ The success of advocacy and campaign communications can only be judged by how they affect an audience. In creating them we must look at what the audience needs, not what we want to produce. To judge the success of a visual executive summary, such as an infographic, look at the degree to which it manages to invite, inspire, inform and resonate with the viewer.

---

9   The master of storytelling with data, Hans Rosling, gives the shortest TED talk ever (blog.ted.com/2012/05/22/). Rosling has a remarkable ability to tell a story with whatever is to hand and this is because the story is the most important thing, the visual tools he uses are just devices that illustrate the point he is making.

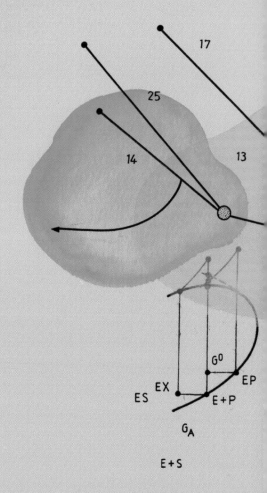

Get the Detail

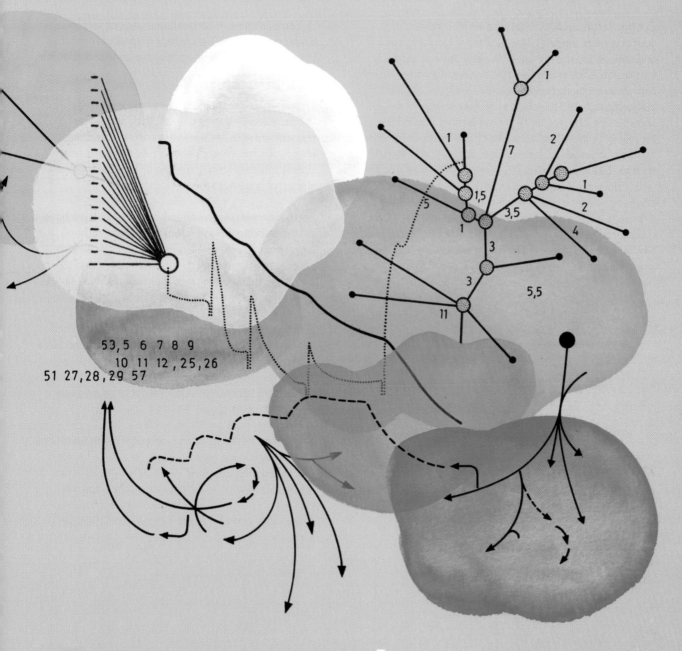

*Journeys
through data*

Get the Detail

The perfect advocacy campaign gives the audience the information they need, in the right amount, at the right time. In *Get the Idea* and *Get the Picture*, we've looked at two strategies for doing this. By using strong imagery built from small packets of evidence, we can draw people in, expose them to our issue and give them an idea of what it's about. Campaigns that aim to help people *Get the Picture* tell stories using carefully selected data to help audiences understand an issue. They rarely include all the information that we have at our disposal.

It sometimes makes sense to give audiences an equality of arms by making an information base available, and thus provide the audience with the same resources that we use ourselves. Publishing detailed information online can have the effect of increasing the credibility of an organisation by demonstrating the depth of its knowledge and creating the air of transparency around a claim or argument. As we have already stated, sloganeering has a limited potential, some audiences need a more neutral proposition before they will engage with an issue. Making information available directly can help nudge people towards you. By creating an open evidence base, we make a different set of offers to our audience: to participate, to invest time; to extend, re-use or add to the information. The art in getting the details is to allow audiences to explore the evidence for themselves to find the stories that mean something to them.

Many advocates are campaigning on problems that are well-known but difficult to grasp. Others are working on issues that are less clear, more complex or harder to pin down.

Initiatives that aim to help people *Get the Detail* are very focused on technology, but we shouldn't get carried away with this. In the design of projects that help people *Get the Detail*, we should ask ourselves why our information is interesting, whether at scale it will stand up to scrutiny, and what role we think visual and interactive design has in our project.

Whether it concerns issues we know about, but don't understand in detail, or issues of which we know little or nothing[1], getting the details is about enabling people to take their own journeys through the information.

---

1   We've appropriated a well-known sound bite from Donald Rumsfeld to structure this section: "known knowns", "known unknowns" and "unknwon unknowns".

Techniques:

A. Exploring "known knowns"

Exploring things that we're familiar with can help to build depth of understanding, particularly in relation to how things work or how they relate to a particular audience. Enabling people to interact with a familiar issue in greater depth serves to deepen their engagement with it. In each of the examples outlined in this section the audience has the opportunity to become a part of the journey, either by controlling the way the data is presented and how it relates to the interests of the audience, or by becoming part of the project by adding content to it themselves.

▶ MAKING DATA MEANINGFUL

Even when governments publish their budgets every year it is very hard for most of us to make the mental leap required to grasp the huge figures involved and what they actually mean. In order for the transparency of government spending to have any meaning it needs to be translated into a relevant form, one that is useful to us. The Open Knowledge Foundation in the UK took the details of the annual government budget, starting with information from the Treasury, and transformed this data into something directly relevant. The result was an interactive website called *Where does my money go?*

Where does my money go? allows users to see the data directly and to map it on to regional spending, but it also makes the data directly relevant to the individual. One of the interfaces, *The Daily Bread*, enables users to slide a counter along a scale stating levels of annual income. On the basis of this it shows the taxes paid at different levels of income, and how they are divided across different spending areas. The site provides details to the penny about how much of the money that people pay in taxes goes to which part of the budget each day. For example, as you can see in the image, of the taxes on a salary of £22,000 per year, £8.00 goes to helping others every day and £4.31 goes to health.

This enables users to break down their personal contribution to running the country, something that can have two effects: first, it connects them more directly to what is otherwise an abstract and invisible deduction of funds from their income; second, it drives them to reflect more substantially on public services that they do not currently use, but may need in the future, such as health and old age services, or unemployment benefits.

RIGHT:
Where does my money go? features visualisations of how an individual UK citizen's income tax is spent by the UK government. Open Knowledge Foundation. 2010.

WHERE DOES MY MONEY GO?

Showing you where your taxes get spent

The Daily Bread   Country & Regional Analysis   Departmental Spending   About

The Daily Bread Costs for the British Taxpayer per Day

SALARY	SELECT YOUR SALARY	YOUR TAX
£22,000		£8,774

Running Government	Defence	Health	Helping Others	Culture	Education	Running The Country, Social Systems	Order & Safety	Our Streets	The Environment
£3.26	£1.69	£5.86	£8.60	£0.38	£1.54	£1.42	£0.78	£0.28	£0.24

Waste	Research into Environmental Protection	Environmental Protection Admin	Environmental Protection	Pollution	Waste water management
£0.09	£0.02	£0.08	£0.02	£0.03	£0.00

WHERE DOES MY MONEY GO?

Showing you where your taxes get spent

The Daily Bread   **Country & Regional Analysis**   Departmental Spending   About

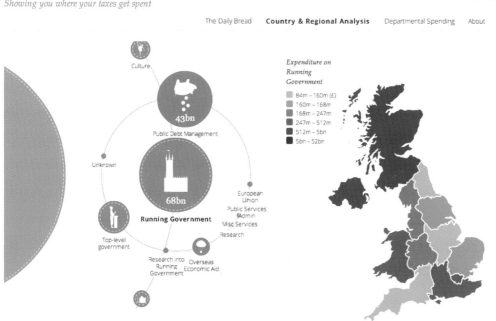

Expenditure on Running Government

- 84m – 160m (£)
- 160m – 168m
- 168m – 247m
- 247m – 512m
- 512m – 5bn
- 5bn – 52bn

Culture

43bn
Public Debt Management

Unknown

68bn
Running Government

European Union
Public Services & Admin
Misc Services
Research

Top-level government

Research into Running Government   Overseas Economic Aid

▶ PUTTING TOGETHER THE FACTS

In some cases it is impossible to help audiences *Get the Detail* without asking them to find the information themselves. This paradox is the premise behind Sourcemap[2], a website that enables its users to construct supply chains and calculate the carbon footprints of common products.

Sourcemap started as a tool to help students calculate the environmental impact of the materials they use in product design and grew rapidly into a platform for public transparency about manufacturing. Leo Bonnani, who founded the site, tells us:

"One of the reasons we have been successful is that people within manufacturing and retail companies have been dying to get data on the impact of their practices, especially environmental and social impacts; they feel like that information has almost been withheld from them. Companies now ask us to help them figure out where they are buying things from and the impact of this, and what that means for sustainability of their products. For me that has been a focus – from the beginning it has been important – because it was about influencing decision-makers: the people who put products on shelves. Across the board I've seen that they don't have access to information to influence their choices better."

Sourcemap also aims to help consumers to better understand the sustainability aspects of their choices by asking them to take their interest a step further and help pull together data that everyone can use. Bonnani continues:

"People want to be able to drill deeper. They are being presented with simplified forms of data. Environmental data is the best example of that. You will have eco-labels on products – like 'FSC (Forest Stewardship Council) certified', 'green' or 'natural' or 'organic'. These are actually very reductive and are data-poor. People don't trust these labels and they look the same whether they are certified and valid or just a greenwashing attempt, like calling something 'farmpicked'."

Bonnani's view is that there is genuine interest in data about how products are made, but the key is the journey that people go through in piecing this together themselves.

"One of the surprises was that people would spend time on the website, browsing and learning and exploring the

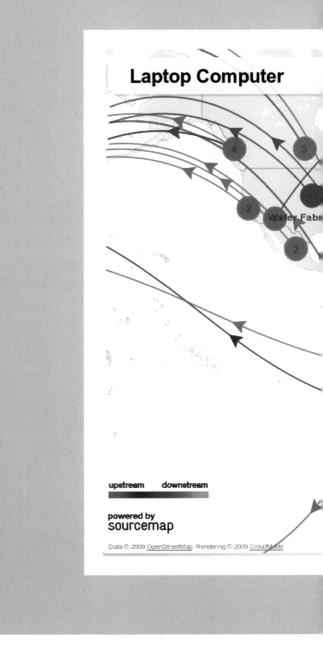

history of products, going through it and seeing the carbon footprint calculations and how they are made, looking at photo slideshows, watching videos, looking at calculations for carbon footprint assessments. So we're trying to replace that reductive eco-label approach with simple online QR [Quick Response] codes that are linking you to a visually punchy story about the product, [something] that you can spend minutes or

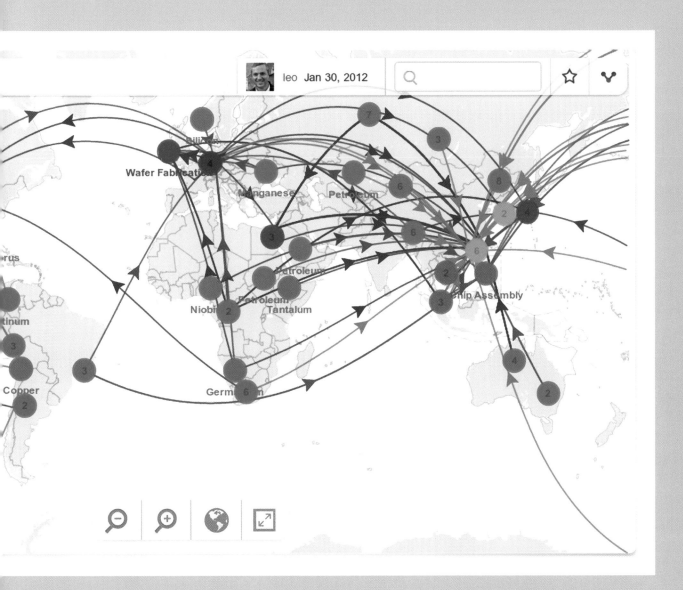

leo Jan 30, 2012

Silicon
Wafer Fabrication
Manganese
Petroleum
7
3
4
8
6
2
6
6
2
3
Petroleum
Niobium 2
Petroleum
Tantalum
Germanium 6
Ship Assembly
rus
Platinum
3
Copper
2
4
2
3

hours delving into. I don't expect that people will know about the impact of their choices unless they really play around with the calculations and visualisations, so it's a learning experience for anyone involved."

ABOVE:
Laptop Computer. Sourcemap 2011. Supply chain of a laptop computer.

▶ FILLING IN THE GAPS

The information that we have may in itself be incomplete. Thinking through ways that our audience can help us with this problem can be a key design principle. An interesting example of this is the *Digital Monument to the Jewish Community* in the Netherlands, created by the Jewish Historical Museum in the Netherlands. The *Digital Monument* is a database about Jewish people from the Netherlands who were killed during the Nazi occupation from 1940 to 1945.

On the website there are personal and family pages for each of the people who died, which include biographical details and home addresses; users can add to this information with photographs and other documents or information they have. This data is made more accessible by a strong search engine and effective data visualisation to help visitors who don't know where to start.

The key insight of this database is that the process of historical reconstruction is contentious and never finished, and that the audience may have the missing pieces. Between 2005 and 2010, the site editors received 28,000

corrections and additions to the data on the site, reflecting the gaps and absences in the historical sources that the site is based on. Eventually, they decided that this task should be carried on through a community-led process, and set up a Community Memorial to expand and improve what is known about the dead.[3]

This example shows that visual information projects that start off as one-way communications of a traditional nature can be up-ended and turned into participatory projects, owned and sustained by a community of users. This approach can be designed for and encouraged, creating a powerful platform where people can invest their time and efforts in curating knowledge about things that they know something about, but want to understand better.

ABOVE:

Homepage of the *Digital Monument*/JHM, Amsterdam, filtered to show the dead who lived in Amsterdam, www.joodsmonument.nl.

---

3 *Jewish Monument Community* webpage: www.joodsmonument.nl/page/484342

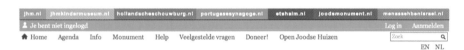

jhm.nl | jhmkindermuseum.nl | hollandscheschouwburg.nl | portugesesynagoge.nl | etshaim.nl | joodsmonument.nl | menassehbenisrael.nl

👤 Je bent niet ingelogd   Log in   Aanmelden

🏠 Home   Agenda   Info   Monument   Help   Veelgestelde vragen   Doneer!   Open Joodse Huizen

Zoek 🔍   EN   NL

Persoon (uit het Joods Monument)

Abraham Goud

Voeg een familielid toe | Alle acties ⊗

Amsterdam, 21 mei 1854 – Amsterdam, 12 december 1941

Heb je extra informatie over Abraham Goud?
Voeg informatie toe »

Abraham Goud was weduwnaar van Heintje Staal. Hij was de vader van Elias, Betje en Sophia.
Stadsarchief Amsterdam, gezinskaart Abraham Goud

In december 1941 zijn in Het Joodsche Weekblad twee overlijdensadvertenties geplaatst voor Abraham Goud.
Het Joodsche Weekblad, 19 december 1941, 9

Heden overleed onze dierbare Vader en Behuwdvader, ABRAHAM GOUD, in den ouderdom van 87 jaar.
Haarlem: 8249
E. GOUD.
B. GOUD—STAAL.
Amsterdam:
Wed. B. POLAK—GOUD.
Zandvoort:
A. GROENEWOUDT.
S. GROENEWOUDT—GOUD.
Amsterdam:
Is. DE VRIES.
J. DE VRIES—GOUD.
12 December 1941.

1636.tif - Het Joodsche Weekblad, 19 december 1941

Op 12 December overleed onze Grootvader en Over-Grootvader,   8250
ABRAHAM GOUD, in den ouderdom van 87 jaar.
Zevenaar:
Wed. E. GOUD,
v. d. HOEDEN en Kind.
Haarlem:
T. GOUD.
D. GOUD.
Amsterdam:
D. GOUD.
M. GOUD—BOOM en Kind.
L. POLAK.
S. POLAK—DE VRIES.
A. VAN MOPPES.
M. VAN MOPPES—GROENEWOUDT.
J. POLAK.
R. POLAK—BEESEMER.
P. STEINDECKER.
A. STEINDECKER—POLAK en Kind.
L. A. DE VRIES.
L. DE VRIES—SCHEFFER en Kind.
FL. POLAK.
A. GROENEWOUDT en Verloofde.
J. DE VRIES.

1637.tif - Het Joodsche Weekblad, 19 december 1941

KLEINKINDEREN Jonas de Vries **HUISGENOTEN** Hartog Levee, Schoontje Sax-Mesritz, Salomon Witteboon, Sara Koster-Jacobs, Betje Cohen, ▪ Betje Vischschoonmaker-Velleman, Salli Scheffer, Sophia Verduin-Hanouwer, ▪ Froukje van der Ven-Coster, Andries Frank, Barend Bonn, Rachel Goudsmit-Barber, Aaltje Ensel-Polak, Meijer Elsas, Heintje Korper-Kinsbergen, Philip Vet, Isaac van der Kar, Judith Vet-Frank, Marcus Blitz, Sophia Os, ⁻ Barend Kornalijnslijper, Gerrit Keizer, Rebecca Krijn-Mauw, Levie Piller, Eva Sons, Vogeltje Leeuwarden-de Goede, Hartog Levie Aandagt, ⁻ Abraham Kroonenburg, Rosette Abraham-Fles, Grietje Goudsmit-van Emden, Rebecca de Haan-Reens, Abraham Hoepelman, Judith Beth-Montesinos, ▪ Isaac van Amerongen, Samuel Aandagt, Dina Abram-Agsteribbe, Meijer Keizer, ▪ Joseph Vos, Hijman Cohen, Rachel Wagenhuizen-van Dal, ⁻ Theresia Kroonenburg-Hartog, ⁻ Joseph Loonstijn, Vrouwtje Mullem-Reens, ⁻ Salomon van Linda, Jacob Groen, Salomon Kijl, Alida Kornalijnslijper-van Kollem, Saartje Blok-Swaab, Sophia Keizer-Krammer, Rebecca Sluis-Gobets, Simon Matteman, Fijtje Aandagt-Gosler, Sophia van Zanten-de Jong, Jacob Rijne, Sara Rooselaar-Wurms, Fetje Halberstadt, Betje Goslau-Bruinvels, Gerrit Appelboom, Sara van Linda-Roeg, Barend Loeza, Kaatje Borstel, Leopold Wolff, Feitje Matteman-Kool, Levie Knegje, Schoontje Werkendam, Elisabeth Juda-Ludel, Clara Levij-van Dam, ⁻ David Sluis, David Visjager, Leentje Visjager-Hond, Sara Waas-Hekster, Abraham Rooselaar, Isaäc Boeken, Roosje Knegje-Flesschedrager, Lea Pront-Snoek, Joseph Scholte, Rebecca Scholte-Gobitz, Hendrika Boeken-Mok, Leentje Engelander-Meijer, Rebecca de Lime, Sophia Groenewoudt-Goud, Sophia Dingsdag-van Amerongen, Elisabeth Stork-van Amerongen, Jacob Korper, Henriette van Dijk, Gombertus Gabriël Duitz, Dora Milikowski, Jochwet Blinder, Estera Stniga, Elsa Emma van Esso-Cohen, Cato Marks, ▪ Betrina Regine den Hartog, Lina van Straten, Greta Vorst-Hartz, Margot Freimann-Hammelburg, ▪ Rebecca Hortence Snuijf, Eva Mina Eitje, Henriëtte Vriesman, Esther Schielaar, Sophie Regina Mol

LID VAN Nederlands-Israëlitisch Oude Mannen- en Vrouwenhuis

WOONDE: Nieuwe Kerkstraat 135, Amsterdam

Print gezin

Binnenstad Oudeschans · s116 Witten... · Wertheimpark · Entrepôtdok · Artis · Van Gogh Museum · Weesperbuurt en Plantage · Frederiksplein · ns · s100 · s112 · Oosterparkbu... · Maurits... · POWERED BY Google · Map data ©2013 - Termini e condizioni d'uso

B. Exploring "known unknowns"

Exploring "known unknowns" allows us to access information about issues we know exist but know very little about. Presenting the details on such topics can help move audiences who are open to a particular point of view but don't have enough information to arrive at an informed opinion or help to deepen the commitment of audiences who already broadly support an issue. Making such details available can help these people to think more clearly about the issue, and may actually move them towards holding a stronger position.

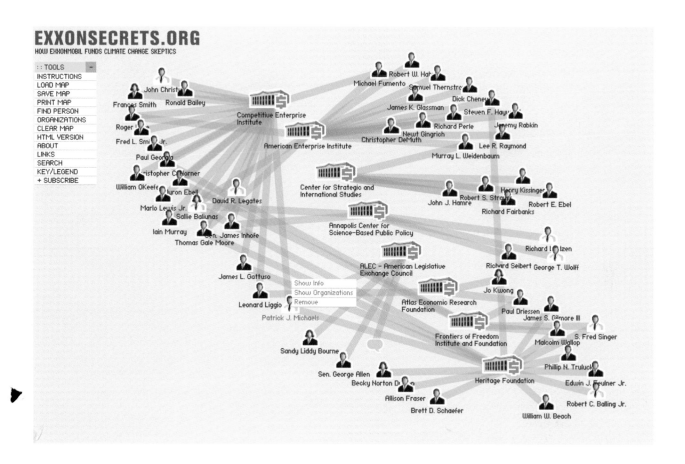

▶ UNRAVELLING CONNECTIONS

ExxonSecrets is a research tool built by Greenpeace.[4] It tracks the flow of money from the oil company ExxonMobil to institutions that have produced research hostile to the notion of climate change. The data about organisations, their funding and affiliations, including statements and public output by the key people who work for them, is very dense and interconnected. It's difficult to understand this in the linear, flat form of tables or even as a simple database. What *ExxonSecrets* does is help show how a political agenda is influenced and supported by corporations. This is a connection that many people suspect but don't know the details of. The image shown here depicts the eight institutions that received the most funding from

ExxonMobil during the time the data was collected. The value of this system as an advocacy tool is to help the user find out for themselves how interconnected thinktank and research organisations are, and how well-organised the movement to deny climate change is. The insight that the designers of this tool had is that most people visiting a site like this don't know where to start, so they created a set of network maps that demonstrate the capabilities of the site while making its message clear. The user can be 'trained' in how to navigate the system at the same time as they are finding out what they want to know by clicking on the individuals and then jumping off from these descriptions to look directly at the source material.

4   Explore the Exxon Secrets site: http://www.exxonsecrets.org/maps.php

ABOVE:
Biggest ExxonMobil-funded climate change sceptics, from *ExxonSecrets*. Greenpeace.

▶ CONNECTING THE DOTS

I Love Mountains is an online component of a larger campaign against a method of coal mining called mountain top removal. Campaigners have been working to show how destructive to the environment and damaging to local communities it is. Explosives are used to crack open a mountain and expose the seams of coal beneath it. Valleys are filled in with the waste rubble, affecting water systems. The website is run by a coalition of organisations working in the Appalachian region of the US, where this form of mining has become commonplace.

For a decade, campaigners had been documenting the extent of mountain top removal using video, GIS and satellite imagery that shows where mining is going on, and presenting images of the mountains before and after mining. With this documentation, giving information about the issue itself wasn't a challenge, but making more people across the country care about it, and do something, was. As with many environmental issues, while the impact for communities near the problem is huge, the impact on the people who benefit from its perpetuation (in this case, energy consumers) can be negligible. So the central challenge for campaigners was to make the issue a national one rather than one tucked away in a remote area. With this aim, the non-profit organisation Appalachian Voices developed the website *I Love Mountains* for the regional coalition, the Alliance for Appalachia, giving the project more widespread appeal.[5]

The *My Connection* tool on the site enables anyone living in the US to see whether the power they use in their house is generated using coal from mountain top removal. For example, if we put in the zip code of the White House, we can see that electricity to that location comes from the Chalktown power station, which has coal provided to it from five facilities that use mountain top removal. Although the visual aspect of this project is fairly straightforward, it's the connection of two other disparate geographies that is important.

The connection tool works by stitching together six different public datasets that cumulatively establish and then present visually:[6]

▶ The location of your house;
▶ The company that runs the electricity grid supplying your house;
▶ The coal-fired power stations that supply electricity to that company and grid;
▶ The sources of coal for those power stations, and the companies that run them;
▶ The sources of coal in the US (and in this case, including coal from mountain top removal in Appalachia).

While the tools used, Google Maps and Google Earth, are commonplace and the visualisation is simple, *I Love Mountains* is a great example of going beyond simply dumping the data on a map. It shows the possibilities for turning abundant data into evidence that can be directly relevant to millions of people at the household level.

RIGHT:
Screenshots from iLoveMountains.org. 2013. *I Love Mountains* My Connection tool creates a map showing how the White House is connected to Mountain Top Removal.

5   You can watch a video case study of the campaign at www.ilovemountains.org/video-resources.
6   The six data sources used in the My Connection tool can be found at http://ilovemountains.org/my-connection#methods

C. Exploring "Unknown Unknowns"

In exploring information that we don't know is hidden from us, the practice of presenting and connecting data is taken one step further, into investigation. This involves piecing together disparate facts about an issue and creating an impression of it that did not exist before. Activists, artists and journalists are often working discreetly, or working against mainstream awareness and understanding of an issue. In this case, the uniqueness of the information being uncovered and the unfolding details about something that was previously uncharted are an integral part of the audience's journey.

▶ PIECING TOGETHER THE FACTS

Questions surrounding the growing industry of digital surveillance have been increasingly discussed in the media[7]; and this is an increasing concern for internet freedom activists worldwide. For years it has been very secretive, and little was known about the actors and its size. In 2012, OWNI and Wikileaks published hundreds of documents on the surveillance industry, working with Privacy International and a number of media outlets, such as The Washington Post and The Hindu, to map this information, allowing readers to explore which companies are making and selling which surveillance tools, and where. The map[8] presents the information in categories such as internet monitoring, speech analysis or GPS tracking, and then allows users to dig down to specific countries and to names of companies and then, from the Wikileaks site, to look at the actual websites or brochures of the companies involved.

7   The Surveillance Catalog, Wall Street Journal, 2012,http://projects.wsj.com/surveillance-catalog

8   Surveillance Who's Who map is available here: http://bigbrotherinc.org/v1

ABOVE:
Screenshot from the *Spy Files* project. 2012. Company details and direct access to technology catalogues, published on WikiLeaks.

▶ UNCOVERING TRACKS

Trevor Paglen is an artist, geographer and writer whose work investigates unknown aspects of American military and CIA operations. As Paglen's work focuses on asking difficult questions about confidential issues, it is driven by the idea that asking the question can be as important as getting the answer.

His project *CIA Rendition Flights 2001-2006* is composed of flight data that he uncovered through a long and diverse process of investigation in collaboration with investigative journalist A. C. Thompson. This was then mapped in collaboration with designer and activist John Emerson [9], giving an impression of the movements of aircrafts owned or operated by known CIA front companies.

The visual aspect of Paglen's work is often intriguing. However, it is the questions he attempts to get answers for, and the negative spaces he tries to fill in, that make his projects particularly powerful. His work starts with important questions that become documented journeys as he tries to investigate the answers. The outcomes of such projects are unknown in advance and this for him is part of the end result. As Paglen says:

"My own particular methodology I think comes out of a background in art, thinking visually, thinking artistically, thinking about what images look like, thinking about allegory, metaphor, that sort of thing. That combined with a PHD in geography as well, so that influences the way that I think about materiality, thinking about how power structures are literally embedded into the landscapes we inhabit, and the places around us."

For the CIA rendition maps project, Paglen gathered data from a wide range of sources, including news reports, amateur flight watchers and direct interviews with pilots who flew the planes listed. He looked for patterns and trends and pieced together details of 'front' companies used by the CIA. The process was captured in a book, *Torture Taxis: on the trail of the CIA rendition flights*.[10]

Some of Paglen's other projects make the limitations of the evidence it is possible to find the centre of the story. These works include blurry long-range photographs of supposedly non-existent military bases, and time-lapse pictures of the barely visible etchings traced by surveillance satellites across the night sky. In these works it is the lack of clarity and the incompleteness of the evidence that strengthens the questions of why it is secret. The absence of evidence becomes the evidence."[11]

9   'Torture Taxis: on the trail of the CIA rendition flights', Trevor Paglen, Melville House, USA, 2006

10   John Emerson was the author of Tactical Tech's first guide on Visualising Information for Advocacy, http://archive.tacticaltech.org/infodesign.html

11   Trevor Paglen's books are simply inspiring: Torture Taxi: On the Trail of the CIA's Rendition Flights, Trevor Paglen, Melville House, 2006; Blank Spots on the Map: The Dark Geography of the Pentagon's Secret World, Trevor Paglen, Dutton, New York, 2011.

ABOVE:

CIA rendition flights map as presented on a billboard poster in Los Angeles. Trevor Paglen and John Emerson, 2006.

ABOVE:
Sichuan Earthquake Names Project, Ai Weiwei, 2009. A still from the film *Never Sorry*, directed by Alison Klayman in 2012.

▶ FROM THE GROUND UP

After the Sichuan earthquake of 2008, speculation and criticism spread across the internet and media about the way in which the casualties were counted and reported and how the disaster was handled by the Chinese government. In response, Ai Weiwei, probably one of the most internationally-renowned Chinese artists, started an investigative project, along with over 50 volunteers, to document the names of each of the children who died in the inadequately constructed schools, the so-called 'tofu-skin schools'. Weiwei detailed the project's methodology on his blog and in one year collected over 5,800 names of children who died.

The image above, taken from the documentary film *Never Sorry*[12], shows the artist in front of the lists that were gathered. These lists were then reused to create various artworks drawing attention to the controversy, such as *Remembering*, a wall of 9000 children's backpacks spelling out statements from parents of children who died. Weiwei conducted his own investigation, and, in an open process documented on the web, challenged the narrative promoted by the Chinese government. By presenting the names of children in simple printed lists like this, a tense contrast is created between, on one side, direct conversations Weiwei and his volunteers had with thousands of individual family members and, on the other side, the lack of regard for these children and their families shown by the state in not creating such a list. As a response, Weiwei's blog was blocked and one of the activists involved in the project was imprisoned. The Chinese government, however, did eventually release a statement and publish an official tally of the number of children who died.

Through spelling out the details with well-researched evidence the artist enables us to get a different impression of the tragedy. Weiwei also raises much larger questions about the handling of national crises in China, the control of public statements and the practices and responsibilities of any government towards its citizens.

Writing in The Guardian about this project Weiwei calls on people to "demand the truth, and to refuse to forget... Question them [the government] every breathing moment. Until our questions become part of the facts." He asks for people to be "... obsessed citizens, forever questioning ad asking for accountability".[13]

---

12   We highly recommend the documentary about the work of Ai Weiwei which tells the full story. More details about the film at www.aiweiweineversorry.com

13   Article written by Ai Weiwei in The Guardian, May 25, 2009.

What can go wrong: the devil in the detail

Get the Detail projects can be tricky to develop because they contain diverse elements that must be brought together: a rigorous and extensive data set, a technical platform to house it, and easy navigability for the audience's different uses of the information. So we need to be able to work with good web developers, information architects, designers, data specialists or statisticians. *Get the detail* projects can take time to design and perfect, but if they work they can significantly transform understanding of and engagement in an issue.

The challenges of designing online systems to help people explore our information and understand our material are twofold. The interaction and technical design of systems is incredibly important, and the investment in technology required to create these sorts of products can be very high. However, even great technical work can't save a project that doesn't have good data, a clear vision of how people will interact with the information and a visual design that helps to navigate the data, not obscure it.

▶ 1. INFORMATION NEEDS TO BE USEFUL AND RIGOROUS

If we are going to present all the information we have, then it is important to ensure that it is reliable and accurate. Any errors are likely to be spotted quickly once information is online – especially by adversaries or those with counter positions – and this could damage the credibility of the project and everyone involved. If we can't solve this problem, then we should make the weakness in our information into part of its character, inviting others to question, add to or verify the information we have.

When we publish all our information and ask people to sift through it, it can start to work like a peer review system. Therefore, we have to be confident about the validity of the information and its source or at least say clearly that we know it is not perfect.

It is really important to have good information to start with. Often people think they have a good data set: they may have collected the information themselves or have taken it from a well-researched report. However, when they start trying to make it accessible online in a more dynamic way, or demonstrate patterns in a visual way, it becomes obvious that their information is either patchy or hard to interpret. If the information is really going to influence the audience it has to be comprehensive and stand up to scrutiny.

▶ 2. PRESENTING INFORMATION IN THE WRONG WAY CAN RESTRICT ITS USE

When we go to great lengths to get information, it's not uncommon to struggle over whether making it public is a good idea. People are often reluctant to share information. If we publish raw information on an issue there is the potential to generate more interest by engaging with those who are also working on the issue or following it. However, it's important to get it right otherwise we can just flood the audience and at times even inadvertently tilt the audience away from further exploration.

Among users, there could be a lot of initial excitement about being able to sort through an extensive set of information concerning an issue they are interested in.

For this interest to be sustained beyond a small circle of experts or specialists, the information needs to be presented in a way that allows people to come up with practical applications or to take the information further for their own interests.

▶ 3. VISUALISING BIG DATA CAN BE AN ACQUIRED TASTE

We have to be prepared to make the visual design useful, and not simply pretty.

Being presented with a lot of information can be overwhelming, and the wrong sort of visual presentation can make this worse rather than better. In *Get the Detail* projects, the visual aspects of information presentation play a supporting role, and not a leading one as they do in *Get the Idea* projects.

Design needs to help people understand the information by revealing patterns and aiding reading. Good visual and graphic design in these projects creates usable filter and search aids that support users navigating the information. Far too many online visualisations focus on ingenious ways of showing huge amounts of information; these can become overly intricate, even Byzantine. Information visualisations that are technically impressive are not necessarily examples of good information or interactive design. Try not to go over the top[14] – users give up quickly if they are not able to interact with the information; this can deter them from staying around very long, or even from coming back.

Finally, off-the-shelf data visualisation tools can be extremely useful, especially when trying to analyse or look for patterns in large data sets, but they also have their limits as ways to directly present information. These tools may be great at helping us organise data in specific ways or to help people get the sense of something, but it can be very hard for users who are not motivated by this form of presentation to engage beyond initial curiosity.

14 *Top Secret America*: Interactive map', The New York Times, 2011.

► 4. WORKING WITH SENSITIVE INFORMATION NEEDS CAREFUL CONSIDERATION

When working with sensitive information, researchers, journalists and activists can find themselves or their information at risk, either when they are collecting and storing information, or when they present the full extent of their evidence on an issue. If the information is likely to be disruptive in some way, then the protection of the information, and (depending on the issue), those associated with it, need careful consideration. This is especially true if the information challenges powerful authority figures, such as law enforcement agencies or public institutions in places where freedom of expression is restricted, or if you are collecting data on powerful actors who work outside of the law; for example publishing detailed information on organised crime. In these cases it can be useful to consider whether there are any partnerships with established institutions that might help to strengthen your position or offer some form of protection, such as academia, media houses, cultural organisations or large-scale international NGOs. Having the right support may help, but more importantly, we need to take careful measures in advance to ensure the safety of sources, the security of the information we are storing and sharing between us, and our personal and direct connection to the information we are publishing.

► SUMMARY: USING DETAIL TO CONNECT PEOPLE TO AN ISSUE

The past few years have seen a shift in the way raw information is used to expose misconduct and increase accountability. In the examples that make up the bulk of this chapter we have been inspired by the new journeys that are now possible, thanks to changes in laws, such as access to information, thanks to experimentation with data journalism by mainstream media and to new tools and platforms and collaborations between hackers and activists. While digital technologies have been central to these opportunities, it's the way that the journey is designed that distinguishes a pointless online data dump from a platform that is an effective support for advocacy.

There are a wide range of reasons and uses, strategic and otherwise, for projects that aim to help audiences *Get the Detail*. They may help persuade people who are initially not very receptive to our targeted communications, by presenting our evidence to them in more neutral ways, or allow those who already know the issue to dig deeper. The sorts of visualisations we can create – mostly online interactive visualisations – open up a range of different ways in which people can engage deeply with our work, whether they are already involved and supportive or not.

► *Get the Detail* projects are useful for taking audiences deeper; substantiating positions and claims, helping audiences discover issues directly and directly, and encouraging people who already care about the issue to deepen their committment.

► Is the information relevant to audiences' professional or personal interests? It can be easier to get people to take part actively, reuse or contribute to data if information is presented to people who already have an interest in the topic. Can the information be presented in relation to the audience's own environment or interests – their community, the country they live in, or the companies they buy products and services from?

► Just building a database and making data public is not enough. Especially if we're engaged in advocacy, we need to think about how the information is contributing to an objective. Even if we simply want to raise awareness or present an issue, there is usually a reason why, something we are hoping people will do with the information or an agenda we have.

► Think about the journey and ways through the data. What kind of journey through the data will help the audience understand it; does it need abstracting and presenting at a top level first for them then to drill down, or would presenting cross-sections or sub-stories draw people in?

Putting it
into Practice

{

This last section, *Putting it into Practice*, is about moving from understanding and being inspired by visual campaigns to planning and making your own. Based on our own experience at Tactical Tech, we share tips and advice on planning and designing visual information campaigns and on telling stories through words and images. We also provide a quick guide to some of the tools you could use and a selection of recommended resources for you to explore further.

The five simple questions you need to answer that will take you through the process of designing a visual information campaign are:

▶ 1. WHAT IS THE AIM?

What is the **change** you are trying to make or the problem you are trying to solve, and why?

▶ 2. WHAT IS THE BENCHMARK YOU ARE TRYING TO REACH?

What are you trying to **achieve**? For example, a change in the discourse, or a shift in the understanding of a particular event or issue.

▶ 3. WHO WILL GET YOU THERE?

Who is the **audience** and why? What form of **intervention** will you choose? For example: **interruption**, **education** or **coercion**? What is their current position and what will nudge or change this? What would change if you were successful?

▶ 4. HOW ARE YOU GOING TO DO IT?

What will get the audience to reconsider or change their position? How will you use **emotional**, **rational** or **moral** appeals to their values and how will you get them to care? What role will the **information** you use play in this?

▶ 5. HOW WILL YOU IMPLEMENT THE VISUAL INFORMATION CAMPAIGN?

To which **networks** will you present the campaign? What **technologies** can you use to deliver the campaign and how will technologies help distribution of or interaction with the campaign? How will the **design** of the information you choose to present support the content? What will be the campaign's communicative power?

Knowing your audience and how to reach them

▶ HOW TO DECIDE WHO TO TALK TO AND HOW TO TALK TO THEM

Too many campaigns are planned with the idea of reaching a general audience. This can be counter-productive, resulting in watered-down communications that talk too generally to everyone without really changing the opinions or challenging the assumptions of anyone.

Creating change through advocacy is often about gaining the support of those who can influence the course of events. It is about reaching them at the right time in the right way. In order to get started we have to make sure we know who these people are, how to target them and what we want them to do.[1]

Tactical mapping[2] is often used in campaign planning: it can be a useful way to understand who is involved in an issue and help clarify who it is we are trying to communicate with and why. Seeing how people or groups on a tactical map fit into an 'allies and adversaries' map[3] can help show whether certain groups or individuals represent an obstacle or an asset and how they are connected. Using tactical mapping can also help in understanding how we can use different networks, the sort of influence we can hope to have on an issue and to help set realistic expectations. The key question to ask is; who are we trying to affect and why, and who can help get the result we want?

If it's hard to get to the person who can ultimately make a decision or a change, or if they are too difficult to influence directly, looking at what capabilities key actors have may help. It's worth asking tough questions in order to come up with the right ideas. At this point going back to the chapter on elements of influence may be helpful. Once you've decided who the primary audience is and have a realistic view on what you think you can get them to do, think about how you are going to get them to care, what form of appeal you will make and what kind of intervention may work given the current situation and the context you are working in. At this point you need to decide what type of information you will use in your visual campaign and why. Test your assumptions – literally try the concept out on others – find out what impression the information you have and the story you are trying to tell makes and see if this is the impact you are hoping for.

This set of questions can help to understand how an audience is positioned and what might reach them:
▶ What is their current level of understanding of the issue?
▶ Why do they care?
▶ Why aren't they doing anything already?
▶ What may change their mind and why?
▶ What influences them? who do they listen to?
▶ What is their communication environment?

---

1   These are the basic building blocks of most approaches to campaign training, there are many free resources covering the basics. Try Chris Rose's Campaign strategy website: http://www.campaignstrategy.org/, or the British voluntary sector resource site: http://www.ncvo-vol.org.uk/campaigning-resources#gettingyoustarted, New Tactics also has a large resource of tactics from around the world: http://www.newtactics.org/toolsforaction

2   New Tactics in Human Rights developed Tactical Mapping and explains it further here: http://www.newtactics.org/resource/tactical-mapping

3   See Tactical Technology's Campaign Strategy exercise From Targets to Tactics: http://archive.informationactivism.org/en/basic1

▶ HOW TO GET THROUGH TO AN AUDIENCE

In order to decide how to design your information and what technologies to use to present it, it can help to put yourself in the shoes of the audience. This involves figuring out how they like to receive information and why.

How detailed your information needs to be, what format it is delivered in and how dynamic it will be really depends on your audience and how you want them to use the information within the visual campaign. Similarly, whether you emphasise capturing attention, telling a story or taking people on a journey through the details will depend on what your audience's level of interest in the information is, how they will use it and what difference you think it will make.

Think about which of the approaches and techniques we have highlighted may work for your issue, the information you have and the needs of your audience. On the following pages you will find a summary of these.

Summary of approaches and techniques

	USE TO ...	WORKS BY...	COMMON FORMATS
GET THE IDEA	Expose	Evoking reactions	Simple graphics and images, posters, simple infographics
GET THE PICTURE	Explain	Telling stories	Infographics, animations, maps
GET THE DETAIL	Explore	Building journeys	Dynamic databases and complex visualisations, interactive infographics

APPROACHES HIGHLIGHTED IN THIS GUIDE	INTERPLAY BETWEEN INFORMATION, DESIGN AND TECHNOLOGY
Juxtapose, Subvert, Invert, Materialise, Compare, Contrast, Illuminate, Provoke, Parody, Intrigue	The visual is the leading factor, often using representation; information is in the background and technology is mainly used for publication and promotion
Associations, Connections, Remedies, Correlations, Portraits, Perceptions, Interactions	Balance of the visual and of information; technology can be used as an essential aspect of this technique, or it may be more important for publication and promotion
Making data meaningful, Putting together the facts, Filling in the gaps, Unravelling connections, Connecting the dots, Piecing together the facts, Uncovering tracks, Working from the ground up	Information is critically important; the visual aspect serves as organising principle and entry point; technology usually plays a strong role

Coming up with an idea

Trying to come up with an idea for a visual campaign like the ones we have profiled in this guide is not that different from any other creative process. This is well-described in guides to creative thinking, but it can be difficult to put into action: the journey we undertake depends more on persistance and creativity than on any hard skills or specific techniques. It's important not to leave the brainstorming for the visual information until the end of the process of working with information – or make it the final step of the process. The search for visual expression of our ideas has to be part of the overall campaign and the way we work with our data. The creative process is a very personal thing, it may take two days or two weeks, but here we describe our journey towards the right ideas.

▶ IMMERSION

We always start with lots of information, data, opinions, needs, initial ideas – and also the hope that we will be able to produce something different. During this phase we try to focus on determining what the problem is. First, the actual problem needs to be differentiated from its symptoms. One way to do this is to ask the question 'why?' endlessly. When we have made an exhaustive list of answers, we can organise them so as to recognise where the actual problems exist.[13] This process helps us check assumptions: **are we addressing the right problem? are we asking the right questions? do we have the right evidence?** This may sound simple, but in our experience of helping people evolve an idea, we have never found a better way to identify and assess a problem and work out a starting point. This method can also be useful to help everyone gain consensus on the overall aim.

By this stage we are already generating ideas. Some will look brilliant and some will look stupid, but there's no need to evaluate them yet, all we do is record them. These are rarely the ideas that we will eventually implement, but this is often when the seed of the best idea is planted.

▶ LOOKING FOR THE COMPASS

This is the time for annoying questions, for searching for gaps in the data or evidence and working out how to fill them, evaluating if any limitations could be turned into strengths. Exploring why something useful is missing sometimes brings unexpected insight. This phase is also about exploring the history of the issue and the problem, how it has been represented in the past, what worked and what didn't. It is time to be playful, pulling together different facts, trying to find the most unexpected ways of connecting and reconnecting them, looking for external contexts for the information we have. At this point it can be useful to meet friends and talk to them about the project; sharing thoughts with someone who doesn't know the problem can force us to simplify our ideas, and may bring new inspiration.

▶ FREE FLOATING

Ideas can come at random, at unexpected moments, and often in the strangest places – paying for a coffee or standing in the shower. There is a certain rhythm to how we function: sometimes to reach that eureka moment we need to take a break and allow our subconscious to sift through the overload of ideas we have amassed. All we can do to help it turn into something is to keep it simmering on the back burner. Breathing space is important: do anything except think about the ideas. Keep a pencil and paper handy. Ideas will come, slowly at first, and then many of them.

---

13   *The Current Reality Tree* is a diagram that helps to identify root causes or systemic problems. See https://en.wikipedia.org/wiki/Current_reality_tree_(TOC)

▶ CATCHING THE BREEZE

If we have succeeded in listening, thinking and being inspired, we should have some strong ideas by now. We won't know yet if they are the ones we will eventually use. At this stage, whether we were looking for the metaphor that would frame the problem in a compelling way, or for the story that would shine a different light on a complex issue, all we need to do is sketch initial concepts. When we feel we are getting somewhere, it is important to show our work to others to test our concepts. Discussing and exploring ideas with other people is one of the fastest methods of iteration and often moves you forward very quickly. At this point we may feel frustrated; perhaps everything starts to look the same. This is great – it's at this moment, when we feel we can't usefully carry on, that we reach our best ideas yet, and things fall into place.

▶ LAND ON THE HORIZON

This is where we move from sketching to realising our idea. We have to be disciplined, rather than just sticking to the idea we like the most; this is not the end of the process! At this point, we have to make a point of being flexible and continuing to listen to feedback while sticking to our original schedule and budget. Things can always be improved, but the main barrier here is the time and resources at our disposal. We have to move forward with our idea and stick to it. Our overall organisational or campaign goals acquire a renewed importance at this final stage, and we should check our concept against them.

▶ WAIT, WE ARE NOT THERE YET!

Things definitely look different when we put them into production. The quality of the material may seem different, the colours may not work, the coder might have trouble doing things the way they were planned, or our testing audience might not understand the way the information is presented. We need to be prepared to tweak our project.

One common mistake is to think that once we have the published item in our hands – a film made or a web site online – this is the end of the process. In a campaign, this point is the beginning! Our project has to get out there and be seen and used, and we have to pay attention to the feedback and responses we get; sometimes this may lead to the original concept and inspire us to adapt it in response to the feedback. We need to monitor our project carefully and be prepared to respond to the needs of our audiences. It's important to respond to the dynamic context in which we're working and to any unforeseen events and changes in the environment. These final adaptations and iterations can help us to meet the expectations we had at the beginning of our project, and to have the impact we were hoping for.

How to tell stories

Once you have decided who you are trying to reach, what you need to say to them and what form you will present the information in, thinking through the best way to package your argument or tell your story comes next. Here we look at three different means for telling a story: animation, data visualisation and infographics.

▶ TELLING STORIES WITH WORDS AND IMAGES

Some narratives are instantly recognisable, as they come from the wider universe of storytelling. These include stories that follow patterns such as 'the crisis and the solution', 'the perpetrator and the victim', 'the symptom and the cause' and 'friends and enemies', and you will have seen some of these at work in the examples in this book.

Many advocates have also been quick to adopt narrative innovations that use complex techniques to build stories, rather than just telling them. A technique that was used in the global climate change campaign 350 and in Barack Obama's successful presidential campaign in 2008 was based on Marshall Ganz's formulation, *story of you, story of us, story of now*. It encourages people to craft personal stories that connect them to the wider community and to the problems a campaign is working on. One way to think about how to use and layer stories with more detailed information is to create a visual executive summary of the main points contained in a more extensive set of documents. This can also create layers of reading, enabling people to explore an issue superficially or more extensively. Giorgia Lupi, an information designer from the Milan-based studio Accurat, calls this sort of presentation non-linear storytelling[5]:

"The big picture is the shape of the story and this must be seen at a first glance. From this high-level view... further levels of non-linear exploration may then invite readers to 'get lost' within the story or stories and engage at deeper levels."

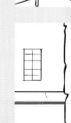

▶ WHAT GOES INTO A STORY

The Story of Bottled Water[6] is a campaign video created by an environmental non-profit called the Story of Stuff Project. This video is one of a number they have made that highlight the social, economic and political aspects of mass consumption and the related environmental degradation.

The Story of Bottled Water is simple. It works to nudge people who may already be unsure about drinking bottled water, but haven't yet taken a strong position, or who have friends and family who haven't really questioned their practices. The narrative is structured to do the following:
- Outline and explain the history and scale of the problem; then,
- Suggest the solution to the problem; and, finally
- Ask the audience for support.

The narrative moves from the specific (our relationship to the problem) to the general (the system of production and consumption) and back to the specific again (what we can actually do about it). The video also has a narrator who tells the story – the prominent environmentalist Annie Leonard. Her persona and style of delivery are central to the video. The story is enhanced by the use of visual techniques, combining a video of the narrator with a black and white animation.

The animation uses humour to underline the main points and keep the viewer engaged:

"The cartoon style allows a comic over-simplification of situations, for example of companies as grinning, top-hatted con-men, highlighting the bare essentials of the networks connecting people, products, markets and government".

The Story of Bottled Water weaves a narrative of villains – bottled water companies – and victims – innocent consumers, of conflict and high stakes. This script conveys selected evidence to the audience and lends credibility to the video's main arguments, citing statements from bottled water companies such as: "When we're done," one top bottled water executive said, "tap water will be relegated to showers and washing dishes". These references are combined with facts such as:

- Bottled water costs about 2000 times more than tap water;
- A third of all bottled water in the US comes from the tap;
- Each year, the oil and energy used in making the bottles for bottled water is enough to fuel a million cars;
- Tap water in the US is under-funded by 24 billion dollars.
  Most of the facts in *The Story of Bottled Water* are headline grabbing, intentionally short and easy to absorb. The distinct facts that the video provides make appeals in different ways; for example, some of the arguments are

based on money, others on health, wrong-doing or market manipulation. The campaign builds on the details in the animation with complementary information on its website – fact sheets, research, annotated scripts – that are available for viewers who want to dig deeper and learn more, or want to adopt or translate the content.

ABOVE:
The Story of Bottled Water. Story of Stuff Project. 2010.

5   'Non-linear Storytelling: Journalism Through "info-spatial" Compositions', Giorgia Lupi, Parsons Journal for Information Mapping, Vol IV, Issue 4, 2012

6   Watch the Story of Bottled Water video at www.storyofstuff.org/movies-all/story-of-bottled-water/

▶ TELLING STORIES WITH DATA

Combining narrative with facts to trace a storyline through data is difficult. Many advocates get nervous at the very idea of telling stories with data. It goes against the principles of working empirically, and we have to be careful not to fall into the trap of shoehorning facts into a pre-defined narrative. Creating a narrative for a campaign from data is a careful balancing act that involves working continually on four fronts at once:

▶ *What is the point?* What is it that we want the audience to understand and why?
▶ *Working outwards from the data:* be clear about what the data tells you. Consider whether the data needs to be simplified, contextualised or completed with other data to make our point.
▶ *Designing our information:* how will we bring our story together in rough data? How can we frame it in succinct and compelling ways without misleading or over-generalising?
▶ *Finding visual stories:* what visual devices can be used to present the information in an engaging way? How can the visual design help organise and give meaning to the data?

If we are very lucky, simply presenting the right data will tell our story and in visualising this it can be the 'raw' form that gives us a sense of data 'as facts' which in itself can be powerful. For example, for his book *The Mystery of Capital*, the economist Hernando de Soto[7] produced a chart to show the large number of administrative steps it takes for a property owner to legalise ownership of their property in Peru (this page, above right). The data about the legalisation process bounce between different boxes, showing the Byzantine nature of the process itself and the unimaginably tedious journey that an applicant would have to make. The storyline is one of astonishing bureaucracy, frustration and complexity. Just looking at the data shows this. And this is only the first of five charts about the same process.

If you are telling stories directly with your data or if you are just trying to understand the data you have, data visualisation tools can be extremely helpful. When you

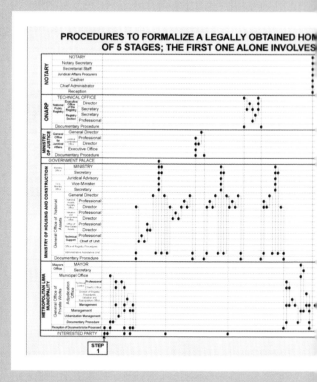

are working with large amounts of information, being able to use data visualisation tools can help you to find and understand the stories in your data.

In analysing social networks surrounding 'La Familia Michoacana' – a drug cartel based in the Mexican state of Michoaca – Eduardo Salcedo-Albaran[8] and Luis Jorge Garay-Salamanca[9] used visualisation tools to map out the nodes in these networks and their connections. The data is based on the statements of witnesses. After looking at judicial files, the team pulled out the details of individuals and their relationships and this enabled them to trace

7   The Mystery of Capital: Why Capitalism Triumphs in the West and Fails Everywhere Else' Hernando de Soto, Basic Books, New York, 2000
8   Find out more about Eduardo Salcedo-Albarán at http://smallwarsjournal.com/author/eduardo-salcedo-albarán-0:
9   Find out more about Luis Jorge Garay-Salamance at http://smallwarsjournal.com/author/luis-jorge-garay-salamanca

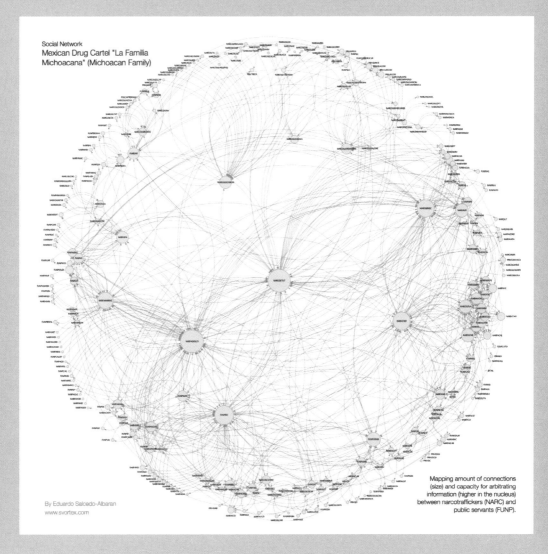

Social Network
Mexican Drug Cartel "La Familia
Michoacana" (Michoacan Family)

Mapping amount of connections
(size) and capacity for arbitrating
information (higher in the nucleus)
between narcotraffickers (NARC) and
public servants (FUNP).

By Eduardo Salcedo-Albaran
www.svortex.com

the extensive social network interacting with La Familia
Michoacana. The resulting spherical network map shows
the relationships between 'narco-traffickers' (mostly the
bigger and more central nodes), and how these central
nodes are connected to public servants and politicians.
The map details 284 agents by name and depicts 880
social relationships. The result is a dense overview of
the high levels of bribery and coercion, and the density
of the network that allows the cartel to function. Visual
representation serves in this example as an effective way
to use the data to tell a story. It gives us an impression of
the strength of the cartel and how it works, and also allows
those involved in the study to get a bird's-eye view.

LEFT:
Procedures to formalize a legally obtained home in Peru – 207 steps.
Hernando de Soto, Chairman, Institute for Liberty and Democracy (ILD) in
Lima, Peru. From The Mystery of Capital, 2000, page 16.

RIGHT:
Mexican Drug Cartel "La Familia Michoacana". Eduardo Salcedo-Albaran.
2010. The map is based on research from a report, 'The Effects of Drug
Trafficking and Corruption on Democratic Institutions in Mexico, Colombia
and Guatemala'.

▶ TELLING STORIES WITH INFOGRAPHICS

Tactical Tech is often asked this simple but hard-to-answer question: "What makes a good information graphic?" The answer depends on what the creator is trying to achieve and who they are trying to reach. However, many issue-related information graphics that work well have some fundamental points in common. These can be put into sequence:

▶ INVITE   A good information graphic provides a concise visual entry-point that at first glance invites us to examine the image further. It gives an initial impression of the issue and creates a quick summary. This is similar to the way we scan a page of text to look for headings and see if it's what we need, or flick through the images in a magazine to find an article we want to read. At Tactical Tech workshops we run 'image galleries', where we find that complicated, dense or technical-looking infographics lose people's interest in the first few seconds even if the content is interesting.

▶ INTRIGUE   An issue-related information graphic that works well often presents something that we weren't quite expecting, or gives us perspective on something out of context. This ignites our curiosity or makes us question our assumptions about the issue.

▶ INFORM   This may seem obvious, but an information graphic actually has to communicate something that the audience may not have known, understood or reflected on before.

▶ RESONATE   Issue-themed information graphics can either chime with or challenge our world view. They can move us away from the visual or aesthetic experience of what we are looking at, into a more rational space of contemplating what the graphic is saying. If stories or statements are implicit in an infographic, it gives the viewer the opportunity to join the dots themselves. This can lead to the final and most important step: leaving the viewer with an open question, or hook, leading them to search for more information, reconsider their views, or get more engaged.

In this visually straightforward map by the Land Art Generator Initiative we can see these four elements at work.

First we are invited to take a closer look by the arresting heading "surface area required to power the world" and a pattern of lines we don't yet recognise on the world map. We are intrigued when we realise that the yellow lines represent locations showing possible future wind farms that would have to be constructed. The infographic does the job of translating abstract numerical information about energy consumption into something concrete. The starting premise for this work was a US government estimate that global energy consumption in 2030 will be 678,000,000,000,000,000 BTU (British Thermal Units – a measure of energy). The project translated this abstract measurement into a 'what if' scenario and mapped this on to a visual concept that we can grasp easily.

At this global scale, the space required still looks small, but at the human scale the potential impact of such a transition would be enormous. Consider the land area that would have to be completely devoted to wind farms. The visual resonates with the audience as it introduces a new sort of trade-off. It neither endorses nor condemns, but asks the viewer to think independently and consider the different aspects of this proposed solution to the world's energy needs. Perhaps most importantly, the graphic raises a more subtle and broader geo-political question, "What would the world look like if energy came from different sources, and how would this draw power away from oil centres like the Middle East?"

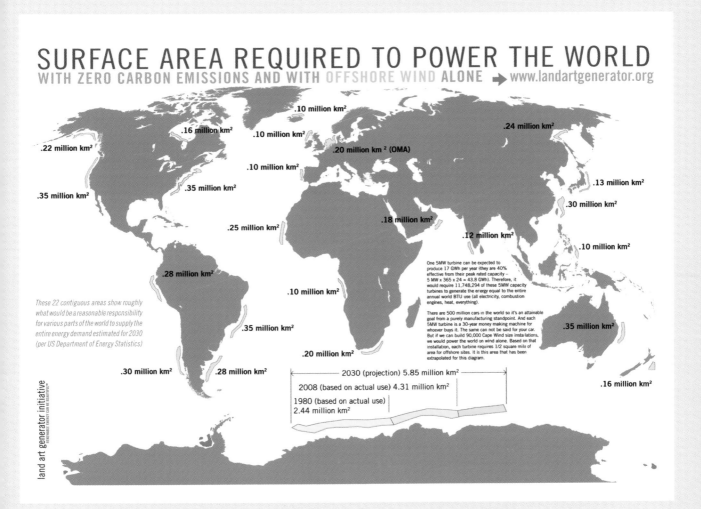

ABOVE:
Surface Area Required to Power the World.
Land Art Generator Initiative. 2009.

Tools for organising and visualising information

There are a wide variety of new data visualisation tools available online. Some of them are free and open source, and others are expensive. Some are simple to use, producing generic images, others are complicated but create beautiful results. Whether you want use these tools to create a graphic, or you just want to use them to analyse your data better, here are some tips on how to get started.

For many people, the first adventures into using data visualisation tools go something like this: use Google to search "data viz tools", read a few blog posts, download a tool, put your data into the tool and watch the "please wait" wheel spin and spin.

You rarely get the beautifully colourful and slick visual you had in your mind's eye the first time round (or the second or the third for that matter). If you are not a coder or a designer, learning how to use data visualisation tools requires investing a decent chunk of time experimenting with the tool and watching YouTube tutorials.

Before you begin spending lots of time learning a tool, it's worth thinking about what else you need to do. Making sure that the visual output achieves what you want means cleaning and selecting the data to be represented and, as we have shown in this guide, having a clear visual concept. You need to think about the most appropriate visual form to represent the data and story – a network graph, map, interactive chart – and what format it will be disseminated in – on a website, in a report, as part of a video, etc.

Here we suggest some tools that you can learn to use with varying degrees of effort. But be warned, there are common problems when using free or open source data visualisation tools:

▶ You don't always own or have control of your data. In some cases the data and the resulting visualisation are stored on the program's website/ server and are public and downloadable. If you are working with sensitive or politically controversial data take care.

▶ Without coding experience (unless you have a coder friend who owes you a favour), those impressive, interactive visualisations with "wow" factor will remain out of reach.

▶ Some of these tools come with a mind-boggling array of options and customisable features. Getting your head round the complexity of the tool and what it is capable of can take a long time.

▶ Take note of what the final format of the visual will be. For example, it may only be embeddable in a website and not downloadable. It may be the case that it can only be viewed on the web as the data is stored online.

▶ A lot of the free, open source tools do not have comprehensive support documentation, forums or intuitive interfaces and are quite simply not as user-friendly as, for example, Google's range of data visualisation applications.

Free tools for working with and visualising data

▶ 1. LIBREOFFICE/OPENOFFICE

Yes, spreadsheets are boring, but for most of us, programmes such as LibreOffice and OpenOffice (or the proprietary equivalent Microsoft's Excel), are what we use to manage, analyse and understand our data. Creating a couple of charts and diagrams in a spreadsheet is a great way to find the trends and stories in your data that you want to visualise.[10]

BELOW:
A LibreOffice spreadsheet using stacked bar graphs to help understand data on the different kinds of violence against sex workers.

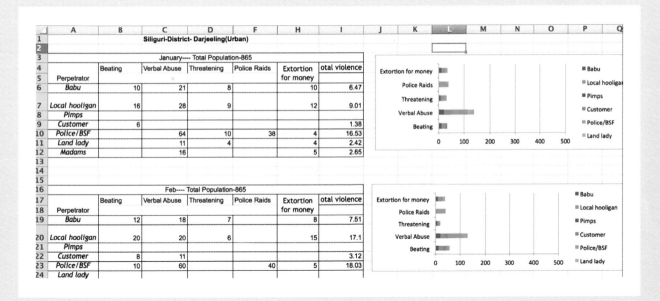

	Beating	Verbal Abuse	Threatening	Police Raids	Extortion for money	otal violence
Siguri-District- Darjeeling(Urban)						
January---- Total Population-865						
Perpetrator						
Babu	10	21	8		10	6.47
Local hooligan	16	28	9		12	9.01
Pimps						
Customer	6					1.38
Police/BSF		64	10	38	4	16.53
Land lady		11	4		4	2.42
Madams		16			5	2.65

	Beating	Verbal Abuse	Threatening	Police Raids	Extortion for money	otal violence
Feb---- Total Population-865						
Perpetrator						
Babu	12	18	7		8	7.51
Local hooligan	20	20	6		15	17.1
Pimps						
Customer	8	11				3.12
Police/BSF	10	60		40	5	18.03
Land lady						

10 School of Data offers online courses on basic spreadsheet skills and analysis, http://schoolofdata.org/handbook/courses/ and Tactical Tech has contributed a course on using spreadsheets to clean data, http://schoolofdata.org/handbook/courses/data-cleaning.

▶ 2. OPEN REFINE

Before putting your data into visualisation software it needs to be clean. This means removing errors and inconsistencies in the data that would otherwise show up and distort the visual you create. Open Refine is a free piece of software that helps you to find and fix mistakes and is especially useful for cleaning large datasets.[11]

BELOW:
OpenRefine catches errors in demographic data from Myanmar.

All	Area ID	Township	Region	Year	Area Total (Squa	Population size ·	Population size
1.	MMR001001	Myitkyina	Kachin	2009	6501.02	25.01	66.12
2.	MMR001002	Waingmaw	Kachin	2009	4877.41	14.12	37.93
3.	MMR001003	Injangyang	Kachin	2009	4776.16	1.09	2.86
4.	MMR001004	Tanai	Kachin	2009	12361.87	5.74	13.38
5.	MMR001005	Chipwi	jachin	2009	3429.4	1.8	4.89
6.	MMR001006	Tsawlaw	Kachin	2009	3509.45	0.81	2.21
7.	MMR001007	Mohnyin	Kachin	2009	6678.35	21.42	61.88
8.	MMR001008	Mogaung	Kachin	2009	2626.17	12.99	41.24
9.	MMR001009	Hpakan	Kachin	2009	6057.67	15.69	38.98
10.	MMR001010	Bhamo	kachin	2009	1965.83	10.22	33.12

▶ 3. TABLEAU PUBLIC

This software for Windows makes interactive charts, graphs and maps from your data. It offers a huge, sometimes overwhelming, range of settings and ways to customise your visuals. It's a good way to explore and analyse your data.

BELOW:
A graph showing WikiLeaks cables by origin made by Neil Houston using Tableau Public.

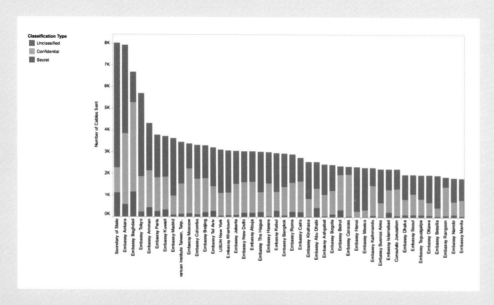

▶ 4. OPENHEATMAP

This tool allows you to create colourful, embeddable maps with geographical data, such as IP addresses, street addresses and longitude and latitude coordinates. The maps produced use different shades and colours to indicate where your data values are larger and closer together or smaller and further apart.

BELOW:
Using OpenHeatMap to show cases of verbal abuse experienced by sex workers in West Bengal, India.[12]

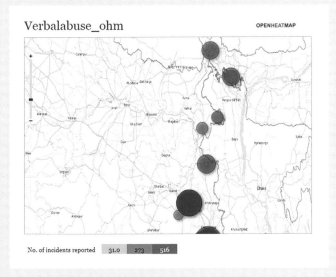

▶ 5. GOOGLE EARTH

Add your own information to on-line 3D maps of the world. You can add text, images, video and audio files to satellite images of the globe, colour areas and even add three-dimensional buildings to the map. You can also explore and animate your content through time and create narrated guided tours.

BELOW:
Johannesburg as seen in GoogleEarth. Add layers of data according to what you want to show.

11 School of Data has an example of how to use Open Refine
http://schoolofdata.org/handbook/recipes/cleaning-data-with-refine/

12 See how we made this map by following our OpenHeatMap workthrough on www.visualisingadvocacy.org.

▶ 6. TILEMILL

An open source mapping tool which turns Geographic Information System (GIS) based data into dynamic or static maps. It gives you more flexibility in the design of your maps than simple heatmaps.

BELOW:
TileMill was used by Nai to map violence against journalists in Afghanistan.

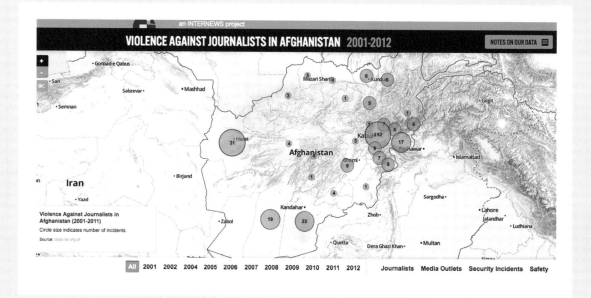

▶ 7. D3

A sophisticated, code-based toolkit that helps you create exceptionally rich and complex data-driven visualisations. However, you need to know how to code. If you do, then this tool can be used to make eye-catching interactive charts, maps or diagrams.

BELOW:
Jan Willem Tulp used D3.js to let users explore urban water usage in different countries, along with quality of life indicators.

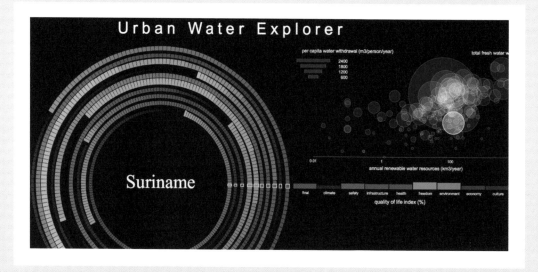

These tools provide a glimpse of what is available. While there are hundreds of information design tools out there, there aren't many that are free, easy-to-use and produce appealing visuals. Choosing the right one is tricky. For more details about tools, look at Tactical Tech's own visualisation and tool reviews on visualisingadvocacy.org where you can explore tools that we have reviewed and tested.

Managing the design process

If you are working with designers, it can be hard to know how to go about this. There aren't any clear guidebooks, and a lot of us learn by trial and error. Here we share insights from our experience of producing visualisations at Tactical Tech and through Tactical Studios, our in-house creative agency for advocacy groups.

▶ OVERVIEW

If you are working with designers, it can be hard to know how to begin. There aren't any clear guidebooks, and a lot of us learn by trial and error. Setting clear expectations at the beginning of the project and agreeing what you are trying to do is essential to producing a successful piece of work. Being both open and clear throughout the process is essential.

The initial project brief is important to set the designer off on the right track. If there is confusion at the start it only increases as the project progresses, and the repercussions can be expensive and troublesome to fix. This is not to say that there is no room for a little creative spontaneity or flexibility in the process, but that the scope, the function and the requirements of the piece should already be decided before work begins with an external contractor such as a designer or a programmer.

Don't delay looking for a designer. Make sure you have time to consult as a team and to get feedback from potential audiences. All of these factors can really affect the project. This is also so that we don't compromise on our ideas because we've underestimated how long things will take, and so that we don't get to the end of the project and find that fundamental elements are missing.

▶ 1. HOW TO CREATE THE WRITTEN BRIEF

▶ **Give the designer a concise description of the project:** give them both a sense of what you are trying to achieve and details of the boundaries of the project.

▶ **Describe your process:** what you'd like to see happening, with specific deadlines for each stage of the process – both for yourself and for the designer. Be clear about the stages of the process, for example, that you want the designer to present three different ideas for you to choose between, or that you need a testing and feedback stage before finalising the design.

▶ **Explain what the essential elements are**, and distinguish these from things you'd 'like to have'. Are there any sensitivities to take into account? Give examples of the sorts of things not to be included, perhaps by referring to other campaigns on the same subject.

▶ **It can also help to give the designer inspiration:** show them the kinds of things you like; use visual examples. If working on a website, collect examples of other websites that you like. Ask the designer to create a 'moodboard', to give you a sense of their ideas before they develop a full design; this can be very helpful for large-scale projects.

What to put in the brief:

- The background of the project, its aims and the issue it is focusing on
- The desired outcomes
- Target audiences
- The main message
- Anything to be avoided in the presentation of this issue
- Examples of the aesthetics, mood, look and feel
- The media and/or formats you'll be using
- Types of distribution, and reach of the project – will you need different versions of the designs to use on different platforms? Will you need to be able to translate any text into other languages?
- Context – is it part of a larger campaign, or linked to a past or future initiative?
- An indication of budget
- Timeline of the project and agreed delivery date
- Any other relevant points – are there any brand or style guidelines? Do you have partners whose input should be taken into consideration?

Thinking about formats:

- **Posters** – even though they are printed quickly, they can linger on the wall for months – especially if they are well designed and beautiful.
- **Printed reports** – are static but tend to be relevant for only a particular time span.
- **Online information** – can be more flexible but readers expect online content to be up to date and to change over time.

▶ 2. HOW TO FIND THE RIGHT DESIGNER

▶ Look carefully at the designer's portfolio; if employing an illustrator, look at their sketchbooks. Consider how their style might fit with the brief. There are different design specialisms, charging different rates: layout for print; layout for digital formats; illustration or graphic design for things such as branding. Try to understand the strengths and limits of the designer and how these match with what you are looking for, as each designer will have a different skill or style.

▶ Help set the designer's expectations. Don't promise them the job if you're trying them out alongside other designers and haven't yet decided which one to employ. Be clear about the process and the payment for any work that the designer does, and (depending on the agreement) pay them at the end of each stage.

▶ If you are working on a large project with a new designer, and you're not completely sure about their skills, set a trial project or period, asking them to work first on a part of the project or a side project, in order to assess whether they are the person you need.

▶ Come to an agreement about process and dates by drawing up a schedule with the designer. This way both sides can commit to a series of tasks and deadlines. However, if the work is relatively straightforward just agree one or two simple review and feedback dates in writing with the designer.

▶ 3. HOW TO SET A BUDGET AND KEEP TO IT

▶ Present a good clear brief so that the designer can cost their time accurately. Agree a lump-sum fee, not a daily rate as that can quickly lead to runaway costs.

▶ If you are changing the brief or the scope of the project substantially while it's underway, be sure to renegotiate, and pay the designer for their extra time.

▶ If the designer doesn't bring up the subject of money or time, make sure that you do before starting on the project and that this is clear and settled before you begin. This can help avoid many tricky conversations.

▶ 4. WRITING A CONTRACT

▶ Put the parameters, the deliverables, the costs and the main delivery dates in writing in a contract. Make sure the contract describes what will happen if the process isn't working, or if the contractor doesn't deliver, as well as specific details about copyright and terms and conditions.

▶ Think about licensing: will this project be released under a closed license, or using a creative commons license? Make sure this information is in the contract, so that the designer understands what will happen when the work is finished.

▶ Tell the designer who the key contacts are, and their roles, as well as when the final verification of each stage of the project will take place, and the final deadline. Prepare a schedule that all parties have agreed to and attach it to the contract with a budget.

▶ 5. HOW TO MANAGE THE SCHEDULE AND THE PROCESS

Open and constant communication is the key to managing the schedule. If both sides have understood the brief and the extent of the work, there's a good chance of fulfilling the commitments on schedule. Problems usually arise for one of the following reasons:

▶ The brief does not give the right guidance – too many revisions are requested too late (perhaps because there is a group of decision-makers which slows down the process);

▶ The brief is changed substantially during production;

▶ The quality of the designer's work is not good enough.

Any of these problems can cause the schedule and/or budget to slip.

It is also important, if working with other organisations (for example in partnership or in a coalition), to understand what makes a successful working process. It is better and more efficient to have one person to deal with on a day-to-day basis. If there are many people involved in the decision-making process, reviews can get confusing and easily create a time lag for the designer. Explain at the beginning of the working period that the views of all decision makers should be managed by one person and channelled through that person at each review stage.

▶ 6. PRODUCTION IS A PROCESS

Production is a process of refining, distilling and improving. It is a reflection of the way we think when we create. Changes to projects during this time are generally positive, they help to perfect an idea. However, you also have to know when to rein them in and get the project finished.

▶ 7. CLOSING THE PRODUCTION PROCESS

Archive and back up master artwork: you may need it later when it may be hard to find the original files, or the designer may move on.

Track how the project is received by the audience, and the impact it has. Write up any lessons learned, for future initiatives.

If there are important things that should be learned from the production process, a debrief is useful for the team that worked on the project.

Keep copies, give versions of the work to the people involved, feature the work on the usual promotional channels (for example online), promote it as widely and get it seen by as many people as possible.

TROUBLESHOOTING

When a production goes awry, it's usually because of one or more of these interconnected problems:

PROBLEM: The design comes back from the designer and it's not anything like what was envisaged or what is needed, even allowing for the fact that it is a draft.

CAUSE: A faulty brief, or a mismatch between the project and the designer.

SOLUTION: Assess whether, with a more focused and better-expressed brief, the designer is capable of handling the project.

If the designer is capable and it is mainly a problem with the brief, improve the brief with more guiding examples and more precise detail, or ask the them what they need to know to improve it.

If, on the other hand, the designer has not demonstrated the skills that can carry the project forward, cancel their contract fairly and offer to pay for the time they have spent on the project up to that point. Try to avoid getting drawn into discussions of design skills.

PROBLEM: Missing a deadline.

CAUSE: Poor communication, bad planning, delay or confusion in the reviewing process.

SOLUTION: With open and honest dialogue with all involved you should be able to foresee any delays. Try and set expectations realistically, and if the timing of the project starts to slip, act quickly by resolving problems, agreeing a new date or getting extra help.

If the delay is to do with the designer: communicate. Ask them to let you know in advance about problems that might affect the timely delivery of the project. If the delay is to do with the clarity of the review process: explain the problem to the reviewer/s and ask them to prioritise and clarify feedback so that you can try to incorporate the changes you want without causing a delay. From this better understanding you can agree a way forward, possibly with revised delivery dates.

PROBLEM: The designer's fee goes over what is allowed for in the budget.

CAUSE: Not communicating well enough; a change in brief; setting a day rate as opposed to a project rate.

SOLUTION: If the brief changes, or the delivery dates are pushed back, the designer may need to charge more for the extra work and time. Renegotiate any extra costs before such changes are agreed upon, clarify any extra charges and try to be responsible when making changes.

However, if the designer has run over the projected deadline for reasons not related to you or your process, negotiate directly with him or her and come to a compromise depending on how much is in the budget and what seems reasonable

Resources

Get the Idea

▶ *Essentials in Visual Communication*, Bo Bergström, Lawrence King, London, 2008.
This clearly written and extensive book is a great introduction to some of the ideas in this chapter.

▶ *Designing for the Greater Good: The Best in Cause-Related Marketing and Nonprofit Design*, Peleg Top & Jonathan Cleveland, Harper Collins, New York, 2010.
24 case studies and many illustrations showing what does and doesn't work in design for notforprofits.

▶ *The Inspiration Room*
A website with a range of different creative and mainly mainstream ways of communicating. The pages organising adverts by brand, including Amnesty International and Greenpeace, are particularly helpful.
theinspirationroom.com/daily

▶ *Ads of the World*
Archives a huge amount of campaign material created by advertising agencies and arranges them by country, media type and industry. It has a section for 'public interest' advertising; the material is mostly mainstream.
adsoftheworld.com

▶ *Social Design Notes*
Is John Emerson's excellent blog about the use of visual communication in activism and is packed with examples and analysis.
backspace.com/notes

▶ *Osocio*
Collects the best examples of marketing for social causes. A great place to find inspiring and slick notforprofit campaigns.
osocio.org

Get the Picture

▶ *The Visual Display of Quantitative Information*, Edward Tufte, Graphic Press, Cheshire, Connecticut, 2001.
Tufte, the 'godfather' of information design, offers a strong and sensible approach to presenting information.

▶ *Winning the Story Wars*, Jonah Sachs, Harvard Business Review Press, Boston, 2012.
The founder of Free Range Studios lays out different approaches to storytelling.

▶ *A Handbook of Rhetorical Devices*
Provides more than 60 rhetorical devices to improve the effectiveness and clarity of your writing.
virtualsalt.com/rhetoric.htm

▶ *The Data Flow* series of books, Gestalten, Berlin, 2008-2010.
Data visualisations, curated and explained and interviews with their creators.

▶ *Information Aesthetics*
A thoughtful selection of interesting data visualisations.
infosthetics.com

▶ *Visual.ly*
Most infographics on the internet end up here.
visual.ly

Get the Detail

▶ **Jakob Nielson's** *"Use-it"/ Alertbox*
Blog provides guidance and tips on usability.
nngroup.com/articles

▶ *Designing Interfaces: Patterns for Effective*
Interaction Design, **2nd edition, Jennifer Tidwell,**
O'Reilly Media, 2010.
Great examples and illustrations show patterns and
best practices for user interaction.

▶ *Big Data Now*, **2012 edition, O'Reilly Media.**
An introduction to the concepts and definitions of
big data, its applications and possible evolution.

▶ *Beautiful Evidence.* **Edward Tufte, Graphics Press,**
Cheshire, Connecticut, 2006.
In the first half of this beautiful book, Tufte lays out
his usual insightful and innovative thinking on
information design.

▶ *Big Data Needs Thick Data*, **Ethnography Matters,**
May 13, 2013.
Tricia Wang defends the importance of stories, social
context and connections between data points in the
age of ever-growing big data sets.

▶ *The New Age of Algorithms: How it Affects the Way*
We Live, **Robert A. Lehrman, Christian Science**
Monitor, August 12, 2013.
Cutting through the big data hype and providing real-
world examples of how big data is used in practice, this
article explores the futuristic implications (both the bad
and the good) of the explosion of data we create in our
everyday lives.

visualisingadvocacy.org
the Visualising Information
for Advocacy site, collates
Tactical Technology guides
and toolkits, offers reviews
of data visualisation tools
and much more.

Extra Resources

▶ WORKING WITH VIDEO

▶ **Video Advocacy Planning Toolkit**
Witness provides best practices and lessons learned to evaluate whether video is right for your campaign.
toolkit.witness.org

▶ **video4change**
Brings together training tools and methodologies from a global network of advocates to support video activists and trainers.
v4c.org/node

▶ **Engage Media**
Is an online video sharing site for campaigners to upload videos related to social justice and environmental issues in the Asia-Pacific.
engagemedia.org

▶ **Insight Share**
Works on participatory video-making, explaining how you and your community can tell your own story through film.
insightshare.org

▶ WORKING WITH MOBILES

▶ **The Guardian Project**
Creates apps and products for android phones to protect communications and personal data from intrusion and monitoring. One of their products, Obscuracam, is particularly useful as it can automatically detect faces in a photograph and pixelate them to make them unrecognisable.
guardianproject.info

▶ **The NOMAD Project**
Supports aid organisations to collect, analyse and manage data collected through mobiles phones. Choose the right technology with their Online Selection Assistant.
humanitarian-nomad.org/online-selection-tool

▶ **Kiwanja**
Collates case studies on the use of mobile technology as a driver of innovation and social change.
kiwanja.net/database/kiwanja_search.php

▶ WORKING WITH MAPS

▶ **Maps for Advocacy**
A guide to using maps in advocacy created by Tactical Tech. Provides case studies, descriptions of procedures and methods, a review of data sources and a glossary of mapping terminology.
tacticaltech.org/maps-advocacy

▶ **Balloon Mapping**
Public Lab explain how to do your own aerial mapping using a balloon, a digital camera and some everyday bits and pieces.
publiclab.org/wiki/balloon-mapping

▶ **Ground Truth**
A blog about community mapping projects and the work of the Ground Truth Initiative which started in 2009 by mapping Kibera, the largest slum in Kenya.
groundtruth.in/blog

▶ WORKING WITH SATELLITE IMAGERY

▶ **The Satellite Sentinel Project**
Uses satellite imagery to monitor and report on human rights abuses occurring in Sudan and South Sudan.
www.satsentinel.org

▶ WORKING SECURELY

▶ **Me and My Shadow**
A Tactical Tech website that allows you to trace your digital shadow, showing all the data you leave behind without knowing it when you are online, and then shows you how to reduce it.
myshadow.org

▶ **Security in-a-Box**
Everything you need to know about how to stay safe online, how to protect your data and communications, and how to set up the tools to do that. A project by Tactical Tech and Frontline Defenders.
securityinabox.org

▶ ## DIGITAL CAMPAIGNING

▶ **The Info-Activism How-To Guide**
By Tactical Tech, provide a comprehensive overview of strategies, digital tools and case studies with a critical focus on the intended strategic impact of campaigns.
howto.informationactivism.org

▶ **The Knight Centre for Digital Media**
Is a great place to find out about the latest new media platforms and tools, attend virtual lectures and take part in tutorials on everything from photography to mapping.
multimedia.journalism.berkeley.edu

▶ **Osocio**
Collects the best examples of marketing for social causes. A great place to find inspiring and slick non-profit campaigns.
osocio.org

▶ **Exposing the Invisible**
A series of short films telling the personal stories of those working at the frontiers of investigation in the digital age.
exposingtheinvisible.org

▶ ## WORKING WITH DATA

▶ **Data Driven Journalism**
Covers developments in data journalism and brings together a host of different resources to help you find the stories in data and visualise them
datadrivenjournalism.net

▶ **School of Data**
A project by the Open Knowledge Foundation, offers a series of on-line courses for people who are completely new to using spreadsheets and to those who are professional data wranglers.
schoolofdata.org

▶ ## CREATING COMICS

▶ **World Comics**
Offers downloadable guides to help with the process of creating your own comic to communicate your message.
worldcomics.fi/index.php/downloads

Acknowledgements and Credits

Acknowledgements

We extend our heartfelt thanks to all the people we have interviewed or otherwise asked for help.

These include:
Ahmed Barclay, Andy Bichlbaum, Chipo Mhike, Christine Kwangari, Crofton Black, Daniel D'Esposito, David Taylor, Eric King, Ethan Roeder, Eva Vozarova, Grace Lile, Icaro Doria, Jestina Mukoko, Kamel Makhloufi, Kersten Nolte, Leo Bonanni, Lydia Medland, Mathieu Boche, Michael Flynn, Mikel Maron, Paul Radu, Patrick Ball, Sally Jean Shackleton, Sam Smith, Sami Ben Gharbia, Shamiso Makande, Susan Middleton, Sushant Sinha, Tim Davies, Trevor Paglen, Yvonne Ng and Zainab Bawa.

Concept and creative direction:
Stephanie Hankey and Marek Tuszynski

Writing and research:
Stephanie Hankey, Tom Longley, Marek Tuszynski and Maya Indira Ganesh.

Design and layout:
Erika Koutny

Cover design and illustrations:
Julia Guther

Image treatment:
Giulia De Amicis

Copy editing:
Caroline Kraabel

Production management:
Lucinda Linehan

Production and research support:
Mathilde Baker, Lisa Gutermuth, Helen Kilbey, Cecilia Palmer, Emma Prest, David Timothy, and everyone else at Tactical Tech for their support, encouragement and patience.

Printing:
Precision Fototype Services, Halasuru, Bangalore

The research, testing, development, writing and production of this guide was made possible thanks to the support of

OPEN SOCIETY FOUNDATIONS

With additional support from:

Hivos people unlimited   OAK FOUNDATION

SIGRID RAUSING TRUST

We would also like to thank our funders and partners who have supported the projects which enabled the development and testing of the ideas within this guide and who have provided support for translations, including IDRC, Indigo Trust and the Ford Foundation.

Credits and copyright

Please contact us for guidance and support if you would like to translate, reproduce and distribute any parts or the whole of this publication (visualisingadvocacy@tacticaltech.org). Please check on the individual licensing details below before reproducing any of the images; many of the photographs and images are the property of copyright holders.

The photographs and images in this guide have been used with kind permission from the following:

Stowage of the British Slave Ship 'Brookes' under the Regulated Slave Trade Act of 1788 (engraving), copyright American School, 18th Century/Private Collection/The Bridgeman Art Library.

Am I not a man and a brother, by Leo Reynolds 2009. CC BY-NC-SA 2.0. Jug from the Norfolk Museums & Archaeology Service.

Glasses from Auschwitz on display at the Auschwitz-Birkenau Memorial and Museum, by Katrina Leno. CC BY-NC-SA 3.0. (https://secure.flickr.com/photos/kate_did/8217351980/) .

Exhibits – 12 Spectacles, exhibited in The Legacy of Absence Gallery, by Naomi Tereza Salmon 1995. CC BY-NC-SA 3.0.

Scared Leaders ad campaign, by Ogilvy Frankfurt for the International Society for Human Rights (igfm.de) 2008. CC BY-NC-SA 3.0.

Facebook You, by Michel Kichka (kichka.com) for TV5 Monde and CfP (Cartooning for Peace), 2011. CC BY-NC-SA 3.0.

Police Brutality, published on Dr Dzul's blog (drdzul.com).

Black Cloud, by Doug Schiff/ Ogilvy Beijing for the World Wildlife Fund (WWF) China 2007. CC BY-NC-SA 3.0.

Cards from la baraja 'Popular', issued at the time of Perón's election campaign in 1951.

Anti-Perón cards, by Juan Jose Ruiz (juanchiomdnew@hotmail.com). CC BY-NC-SA 3.0.

Khede Kasra campaign, by Leo Burnett Beirut for the Hariri Foundation 2009. CC BY-NC-SA 3.0.

A year in expenses & *Table of Expenses*, by The Guardian datablog 5 February 2010, copyright Guardian News and Media.

The Land Matrix, by The Land Coalition in partnership with Tactical Tech, 2012. CC BY-NC-SA 3.0.

How to starve to death on a full stomach, by Susan Middleton (photograph of stomach contents, 2005, CC BY-NC-ND 3.0)/ David Liittschwager (photograph of albatross chick, copyright 2005), Publicis Mojo Auckland, for Greenpeace 2007.

We Agree, by The Yes Men/Rainforest action Network/Amazon Watch 2010.CC BY-NC-SA 3.0.

Adopt a Chevron Board Member, screenshot from the *We Can Change Chevron* campaign, by Rainforest Action Network.

Bahrain land shots, by anonymous internet activists 2006. CC BY-NC-SA 3.0. (Maps copyright 2006 Digital Globe/Europa Technologies/Terrametrics/Google).

Rose, by Yasin Lekorchi and Malin Akersten Triumf, photo Niklas Alm/Vostro, retouch Sofia Cederström/Vostro, Volontaire, Sweden (www.volontaire.se) for Amnesty International, Sweden 2009. CC BY-NC-SA 3.0.

Adopt a Child, copyright Tulika Tagore (concept and art direction)/EuroRSCG India 2008, for Children of the World (India) Trust.

Meet the world – Brazil, by Icaro Doria/FCB Publicidade, for Grande Reportagem 2005.CC BY-NC-SA 3.0.

Meet the world – Somalia, by Icaro Doria/FCB Publicidade for Grande Reportagem 2005.CC BY-NC-SA 3.0.

Meet the world – China, by Icaro Doria/FCB Publicidade for Grande Reportagem 2005.CC BY-NC-SA 3.0.

Children's map of the world, copyright Linus Östholm and Fredrik Lund/DDB Stockholm for Save the Children, Sweden 2009.

21st December 2012, Hassu Khel, North Waziristan, Pakistan & *3rd January 2013, Almsanh Bakifa, Yemen* by James Bridles/James Bridle's Dronestagram blog 2012/2013.CC BY-NC-SA 3.0.

Drone Shadow 002, Kemeraltı Caddesi, Istanbul, 09/10/2012, by James Bridle. CC BY-NC-SA 3.0.

Middle East – who backs an immediate ceasefire? Copyright The Independent 2006.

Function, by Kamel Makhloufi 2010 (blaste.net).CC BY-NC-SA 3.0.

Across the wall, by Visualizing Palestine 2012. CC BY-NC-ND 3.0.

Is this yours? Copyright Greenpeace/Alex Hofford 2007.

Ken finds some hard truths about Barbie, copyright Greenpeace 2011.